Held Togetl

Held Together

AN EXPLORATION OF COHERENCE

Michael Adie

FOREWORD BY
Susan Howatch

DARTON·LONGMAN + TODD

First published in 1997 by
Darton, Longman and Todd Ltd
1 Spencer Court
140–142 Wandsworth High Street
London SW18 4JJ

ISBN 0–232–52190–5

A catalogue record for this book is available
from the British Library

Acknowledgements

Thanks are due to the following for permission to
reproduce copyright material: Faber and Faber Ltd for
'The Dry Salvages' from *Four Quartets* by T. S. Eliot;
Macmillan for extracts from *Experimenting with an
Amen* and *The Echoes Return Slow* by R. S. Thomas.

Phototypeset by Intype London Ltd
Printed and bound in Great Britain by
Redwood Books, Trowbridge, Wiltshire

Contents

Foreword by Susan Howatch vii

Preface 1

1 A Fragmented World 4
2 At One with the World 15
3 The Man of Integrity 29
4 Encouragement 44
5 Held Together 59
6 Entering God in Prayer 73
7 Being Together 89
8 Holding Together 103
9 Drawing the Threads Together 118

Appendix 132

Foreword

THIS is both an intensely modern and an intensely traditional book. It is modern because it wrestles with one of the biggest cultural and spiritual challenges confronting today's society: the fragmentation of culture and spirituality themselves into what is widely perceived as dangerous chaos. It is traditional because it suggests for this mass disorientation a remedy which is grounded in history and practical experience: the Christian faith and life, both of which are rooted in the idea of coherence. As the millennium hurtles to meet us and the fissures in society deepen, how timely it is to be reminded in this book that there is an alternative to fragmentation, alienation and despair! Christianity teaches that there is nothing so broken that it cannot be mended, refashioned and redeemed.

The author of *Held Together*, Michael Adie, was the Bishop of Guildford from 1983 until 1994. Earlier in the century Hensley Henson wrote: 'A bishop, I remind myself, is not quite as other men', and after reading this book I could only think: 'Vive la différence!' I had encountered a wisdom which could only have been acquired by years of pastoral experience honed by a searing spell as a Christian leader at the cutting edge of reality. Written in plain, uncomplicated language, the book speaks lucidly of our complicated times and the complex, timeless truths which illuminate them.

The bishop describes his book as 'theology on the hoof', but I would prefer to describe it as 'Anglicanism with wings' – quintessential Anglicanism, the best kind, which soars far above faction-fighting and fanaticism in a humble, scholarly and profoundly humane quest for truth. In this book the voice of Anglicanism sings out with the power of a mighty bell ringing true.

Yet the Anglican tradition itself is in the grip of the urge to fragment, and like the society it serves it is in urgent need of healing. The bishop has experienced the turmoil; he was recently in the front line of one of the Church of England's most bitter internal disputes, but his 'theology on the hoof' reminds us that Christianity is not only a religion of hope but a transforming, integrating force. We are held together in the Trinitarian God who expresses unity in diversity, and in being God-centred instead of self-centred we can achieve healing and wholeness.

I commend this book to all those people, Christian or otherwise, who are concerned about the nihilism of the *Zeitgeist* and who wish to hear of a more realistic approach to the rewards and challenges of being alive at the end of the twentieth century. Michael Adie writes: 'The sure mark of an integrated person is not only that he is self-aware and at ease with himself, but that he is glad and grateful for being who and what he is, in spite of shortcomings and failures.' The road to integration – of fulfilment and lasting happiness – is often hard to find, particularly today when lack of integrity is rife, but *Held Together* is a most welcome guide-book as we struggle forward on our journey.

SUSAN HOWATCH

Preface

MY experience of everyday work is that it is made up of a scattered collection of bits and pieces. When I was working full time, the demands were such that there seemed little obvious continuity. I felt I was often having to move from one specific task to another, which was quite unrelated to what I had just been doing. Furthermore, I was always aware that I was at the mercy of events: I spent too much time responding to the demands people and circumstance imposed on me, rather than making the space and time to determine my own programme and set my own priorities. When my responsibilities increased, I imagined I should gain more control over my diary and be more in command. I was wrong. As my responsibilities grew, my control of the diary diminished: I found that circumstances frequently required me to reschedule arrangements at short notice. These repeated changes exacerbated the sense of my work being fragmentary. In all this I do not think I was different from many people in other walks of life; they too seem to feel life is fragmented.

Retirement has now allowed me more freedom and provided the space to think back over the way that for more than forty years of work I found it hard to hold on to any sense of coherence in what I was doing. I knew there was a cohesion, but that knowledge was more in the mind than in the heart – an intellectual conviction rather than any consciously enjoyed sense of completeness. Now, with more leisure at my disposal, I have reflected on this sense of busyness and the fragmentation which beset so many of us, and tried to work out more coherently where our true integration lies. I now offer the thoughts set out here in the hope that they might be of some value and use to those whose experience has been in some measure parallel to mine.

I have especially in mind those who sit in the pews of our churches wanting to make more connections between the traditional liturgies of the church, which at times seem to come from another world, and their day to day experience of home and work. Equally I have in mind others who do not sit in pews but who sometimes ponder whether they might venture there if they could first see some way in which their experience of life is related to what they see of the church. My hope is that this small book may make some connections.

In a sense the book itself reflects the very fragmentation that I have long wanted to overcome. I have not the mind or the brain to write with any polished learning or rounded scholarship, and what is offered here makes me recall the curious word that is used in the Acts of the Apostles (17.18) where St Paul is criticised for being a 'babbler'. The Greek word used is *spermologos*, which means strictly a picker up of odds and ends – a bird which picks up seeds at random, not always ensuring it has a balanced diet. So the word comes to mean a person who picks up scraps of knowledge – a babbler. If this book reads as though it is written by a picker up of odds and ends, I am neither surprised nor ashamed. Theology (which is only the formal name for thinking about God) is not best done in ivory towers, whether academic or episcopal, but on the hoof and in the market place.

This book is theology on the hoof. It makes few claims for itself because it patently draws on the wisdom of others, many of them named. Others remain unnamed although my debt to them, remembered or forgotten, is profound because such insight as is presented here is quarried from other and better minds. Among those for whose encouragement and criticism I am indebted are Kenneth Stevenson, who pressed persistently that I should try my hand at writing, Donald Allchin and David Wilcox, who were generous of their time in reading an earlier draft and making criticisms and suggestions, and Morag Reeve, who has guided and encouraged me through the labyrinth of publishing.

If birds pick up odds and ends of seeds and in doing so do not always achieve a balanced diet, it is equally true that bees move from one flower to the next, gathering fragments of nectar which they then digest into the elixir of honey, which carries the rich and accumulated flavour of the flowers.

If what I have written comes anywhere near an elixir, I hope it will be not just an elixir of honey but that Elixir of which George Herbert wrote in his poem of that title:

> Teach me, my God and King,
> In all things thee to see,
> And what I do in anything,
> To do it as for thee.

1

A Fragmented World

EARLY in 1993 England paused. James Bulger, only two years old, had been abducted and murdered by two boys not yet teenagers. The event made the nation catch its breath, and for a time we stopped and wondered. Our society appeared to be crumbling in our hands, and we had to ask whether we had lost our way. Had moral standards so wholly evaporated that two boys so young could in broad daylight embark on a deed so dark? Had society, not least its families and schools, failed our young people by not enabling them to see their potential both for good and evil? Did this appalling act symbolise the disintegration of our society?

There had been stark tragedies before 1993 as there have been acts of mad obliteration since. In 1966 116 children lost their lives in a landslip at Aberfan, and this must have been due to human error and carelessness. At Hungerford in 1987 sixteen people were murdered by a gunman who lost all sanity; and a parallel tragedy at Dunblane in 1996, when sixteen children and their teacher were shot dead, was yet more tragic because all but one of the victims were small children.

These and other acts by people who have morally or mentally disintegrated have shaken us, yet it was the abduction and murder of a toddler by boys who were ten years old which brought us to a standstill because the perpetrators of this atrocity were so young. All human beings can at times be unpredictable in their behaviour. There will always be odd individuals who spin out of moral and physical control. But when such young boys in cold blood do such a deed, we can no longer shrug it off as 'one of those things'. We had to pause and ask where are we as a society going? Is our society disintegrating? Are we, perhaps barely consciously, a part of such disintegration? Are we not just seeing breakdown in moral standards, but finding within ourselves the seeds of a larger fragmentation which affects us as individuals and as a community? The break-down so tragically symbolised by the murder of James Bulger provoked many into thinking further about the lack of coherence in ourselves and in our society.

I

Once a week many streets are dotted with black sacks waiting for collection and disposal. The thin plastic strains to conceal irregular shapes and the jumble of bits and pieces which stretch and distort the sack. These discards of life are cluttered and random, and those misshapen black sacks are a symbol not only of a throw-away culture but of a life and society which are higgledy-piggledy and fragmented.

Our experience is that life often seems like a black sack – a random collection of items which we cannot easily hold together. In a typical working day we might embark on a multitude of activities – answering some letters, seeing our boss about a problem, attending a time-consuming (and usually ill-organised) committee. At home we might read a book, until interrupted by a telephone call; embark on a DIY job, until someone rings the front door bell; and then watch the television news covering a cascade of events across the world. At the end of any day when we look back over what we have done, we see hours that have been packed and filled, but with a jumble of bits and pieces, and we puzzle to find any coherence. What do all these bits and pieces add up to at work or at home? How in any case do these two parts of our life, employment and leisure, fit together? Where, in the end, are we getting to? Each of our separated activities is no doubt in itself worth while, yet there is little cohesion.

This personal experience is reflected more widely in society as a whole. Class distinctions are less evident than fifty years ago, but many still detect a hidden snobbery which assumes, if not class divisions, at least a sliding scale of economic groupings. We have been made aware also of the disintegration of the family, of the increase in single-parent families, of the large number of children now being reared in one-parent homes. There are few families now which have wholly escaped the ruptures of a broken marriage close to home. Then we hear repeatedly that we are a pluralist society with competing religions and cultures. Even though such comments need a careful critique before we blandly accept them, there still remains enough evidence to justify the conclusion that society, with its mix of creeds and colours, mirrors the lack of integration which we experience individually.

We also have to recognise that there are divisions in ourselves that we do not always acknowledge or identify. We have at times painfully to discover that we are prejudiced without having been aware of it. The black community, for instance, has steadily pointed out the sense of racial superiority that lurks in the white mind, and we are often surprised to be told how some of our remarks and actions unconsciously reveal what to them appears to be a mental imperialism. Women have strenuously asserted that there are male presuppositions in many attitudes of society and of individuals, and so they too have challenged our assumptions of peace and harmony.

Our society not only pushes us in this direction, but conditions us into thinking this is normal, even satisfactory. Much of our culture is constructed on the adversarial principle, such as in parliament or the courts. The Houses of Parliament are built with benches opposing one another, and so structure confrontation. The courts work by the adversarial method and rely on cross-examination. This can be a crisp and rigorous method of argument and may be suited to politics and the law, but we have too readily as a society assumed that it is the normal and best method of grappling with all issues. The legacy of 'conviction politics' has accentuated this. The elevation of mental certitude and the refusal to countenance an alternative ('there is no other way') to almost a moral quality has embittered controversy and reduced the scope for reasoned consensus.

The media seem to think that as part of their effort to be fair to both sides they should create another side even if there hardly seems to be one. They polarise every debatable issue. So they relish opposing one point of view with another, and headlines love controversy. Without always recognising it, we are conditioned into assuming that this is and must be a divided society.

We have for some years been living in a culture of privatisation – although there are signs that society is no longer convinced that it is quite the magic solution that we were once told. Whatever the social or economic gains of privatisation, it gnaws away at any sense of national coherence. We now have not so much a National Health Service as a spread of separate trusts, working to a common pattern perhaps, but in some measure in competition. We have a national educational system, but it is more divided than it was, with schools being encouraged to go it alone. It is less clear than it used to be that they are all working together as part of a coherent system. Competitiveness has many merits but, unbridled, it can damage or destroy co-operation and cohesion.

Alongside this privatisation, and in some measure as a result of it, religion is seen less as public truth than as private opinion. Belief, once seen as opposed to unbelief, is now contrasted with knowledge, so that if you stop to ask whether this is the right road to London and receive the answer 'I believe so' you are left in some doubt. Belief, it is commonly assumed, is a matter of individual choice, and religion is a hobby for those who like that kind of thing, although others, of course, prefer badminton or rambling. And people talk (too easily and unthinkingly) about our being a pluralist society, as though that were a fact of life which we are powerless to change, nor should we search for a way to do so.

It might be alleged that this emphasis on a sense of fragmentation is exaggerated and is in the mind of only one isolated individual. That does not seem to be so. Bishop Kenneth Stevenson, for instance, in his enthronement sermon at Portsmouth in 1995 referred precisely to this limitation to the attaining of any full sense of our true humanity. He refers explicitly to the fragmentation and brokenness which people in our society experience:

> Many people can no longer see their lives as whole, as united, as in some kind of continuity. The quest for this beating heart of love at the centre of the universe, which we can call God, or meaning, or truth, is about taking those brokennesses seriously and not trying to resolve them in such a way as to pretend they never existed. We are all scarred by life, to a greater or lesser extent. But perhaps what only adds to the pain of brokenness is that we somehow know deep within ourselves that we are meant to be 'whole', and that disintegration is really only a phase on the road to integration.[1]

II

This sense of fragmentation, it must be said, is not just a recent experience, and we cannot attribute all its evils to the modern generation of politicians. It runs deeper than that and is of longer standing. St Paul wrote of being all things to all people[2] – a phrase which has crossed over from the Bible to become part of everyday idiom. He meant that positively: he was able to stand by each person in his or her personal position and ensure that the gospel engaged with their particular circumstances,

hopes and fears. But there is a knife-edge distinction between
that and just being fickle – changing our attitudes, approaches
and stances according to immediate circumstance in a way that
leaves us lacking consistency. George Herbert encapsulates this
with his usual economy of words:

> Oh, what a thing is man! how far from power,
>   From settled peace and rest!
> He is some twenty several men at least
>   Each several hour.

It is worth noting here that Herbert in his last stanza in the
poem knows where to turn in hope of integration:

> Lord, mend or rather make us: one creation
>   Will not suffice our turn:
> Except thou make us daily, we shall spurn
>   Our own salvation.[3]

The French Jesuit, Auguste Valensin, wrote in his journal:

> How complex man is! I feel that I could in all sincerity, talk
> successively to several people in a completely different way –
> that I could be a conservative, then liberal, that I could appear
> timid, and then bold – reactionary, and then modernist – which
> of these is the real I? Often I have no idea.[4]

Thomas Hardy was well aware of the human being's struggle
for integration. He noted on 2 January 1888:

> Different purposes, different men. Those in the city for money-
> making are not the same men as they were when at home the
> previous evening. Nor are these the same as when they were
> lying awake in the small hours.[5]

And two years later Hardy still had this in mind but in more
general terms:

> I am more than ever convinced that persons are successively
> various persons, according as each successive strand in their
> characters is brought uppermost by circumstances.[6]

This was the period when Hardy was creating such characters as
Henchard in *The Mayor of Casterbridge*. One reason why Henchard is such a compelling tragic hero of the novel is because
for all his diverse failures we know how we share his disintegration and so we identify with him and cannot wholly
condemn him. With sure dramatic power Hardy allows Henchard to find final integrity only when he solemnly in his last

signed statement insists on total annihilation – with no grave in consecrated ground, no sexton, no mourners, no memorial. This last wish is respected by Elizabeth Jane precisely because she knew that Henchard had at last meant every word of it. This desperate final stroke for integrity is nihilistic in Hardy's hands, but it is dramatically powerful nonetheless, and gives a sure insight into our deep and desperate need to find cohesion in our being.

In a totally different and strongly theological context Leonard Hodgson touched on this unavoidable element in our make up:

> Most of us know what it is to be torn in different directions by different elements in our personality; we know what the psalmist meant when he wrote 'With the pure thou shalt be pure, and with the froward thou shalt learn frowardness' . . . When the day is done, and we look back over it, and see this creature dragged hither and thither by this interest and that, we may well ask, 'Which of these things is the real I?' Am I really any*one* at all?[7]

So this experience of lacking any consistency in ourselves is not the sneaking quirk of an individual, nor a new found strand in the make up of the modern generation. Perhaps the reality is that we feel it more acutely than did our predecessors because we see it writ large across the headlines and hoardings of our society. But it has always been there.

The way that the world impacts on our awareness reinforces this sense of fragmentation. Our experience of this world is that we are bombarded by fragments of it through the media and through our encounters with other people. It is not easy to experience the world as a coherent whole. Austin Farrer, thinking in philosophical terms, said that we do not experience *the* world as a unity:

> The universe isn't *an* organism, or *a* system or *a* process: it's an unimaginable free-for-all of innumerable bits of organism, system, process: or, if you'll allow me an antiquated piece of slang, it's not a thing, it's just one damned thing after another.[8]

Modern art in its post-modernist form seems to bombard us with a host of images, placing side by side symbols of previous styles and forms as though each and every image can be equally employed and presented without coherence, and without looking through to any integration in reality. In post-modern literature and philosophy there is reference, significantly, to 'deconstructionism' as though there is artistic merit in destroying coherence.[9]

It is perhaps because we have lost any sense of integration in life and in society that much of the western world has in recent years become preoccupied with integrity, or the lack of it, in public life – hoping somehow that if we could restore it there, then it would trickle down into our society as a whole. The English have always held 'sincerity' as a treasured personal quality, wanting their heroes to practise what they preach. Now there is much talk about the lack of integrity of those in public life, and politicians and other public figures are hounded off the stage into the wings because in the glare of the media spot lights we can see their private life does not cohere with their public statements. This has become almost a crusade, as though sub-consciously we are yearning for some integrity and integration in our life and hardly know how to establish it.

This brokenness and lack of integrity, which we experience both in our society as a whole and as individuals, is of course apparent in the church. There is the tragic division of Christendom into East and West since 1054. There is the crumbling of the western church at the Reformation. There are divisions within our churches today, to which we have become so accustomed and acclimatised that they no longer shame us – almost the reverse: many people in our consumer society assume that there should be variety of choice in a religious supermarket and we should have a right to select the style of worship, the set of doctrines, and the kind of priest that suit our preference. During the twentieth century there has been impressive if slow progress towards Christian unity and most churches now recognise that they have more in common that holds them together than differences which force them apart, yet much of the ground gained is at risk because in the last few years of the century there has developed a culture of private choice at the cost of loyalty to the community, an elevation of consumerism at the expense of the Christian duty to remain one body.

III

This sense of brokenness and the disintegration of ourselves and of society is not the only issue of concern facing us today, and it must be seen in perspective, not least in a society which has conceded too much to those who pursue single issues. We have seen groups objecting to bypasses which damage the environment, groups who object to the dumping of oil-platforms in the sea because of the risk of damage to the ocean, groups championing the rights of animals, and many others. They may be right or not in the case they press, but in presenting their cause they seem to ignore the possibility that there are other considerations, and other causes equally valid. They are crusaders, and it is not the style of crusaders to consider an opposite point of view. We hope to avoid the crusading error, and recognise that there are many and other aspects of contemporary life which cry out for recognition and remedy. The underlining of fragmentation here is drawing attention to but one significant aspect of contemporary life. But engaging with it may give us a way in to considering not only this but other contemporary anxieties and so to enter more fully the Christian traditions that we have inherited.

In any event, this experience of fragmentation and lack of cohesion in society and in the church must be confronted or we shall increasingly accept fragmentation as the norm. We must try to find a way through, a pattern of life which enables people to discover that integrity and cohesion which we so patently lack at the present time. So we note at once that Christian faith and life are rooted in the idea of coherence. God is one. That God of unity has entered and engaged with this world to bring reconciliation. He shared our life with us that we might share his life with him: the purpose of the life and ministry of Christ was to draw us into the life of God and he has entrusted us to make that reconciliation effective in a disintegrated world. The whole thrust of God's work can be seen as a divine determination to draw us together in him, and God rashly invites us to engage in that unifying movement.

IV

It might seem that this is a task wholly beyond us, and surely even when we dig deep into our inner resources and draw on the strength of God it will not be easy, because we are wrestling with a stubborn aspect of humanity. Humanity is not only divided but often wants to be divided. That is writ large in southern and eastern Europe at the present time, as we see nationalist communities almost revelling in being at loggerheads with one another. Tribalism runs deep in most human communities. Our disintegration needs not just gentle healing but incisive surgery. William Temple, writing in November 1939 when the dark cloud of aggression was rolling across Europe, warned us:

> We cannot come to the men of today saying, 'You will find that
> all your experience fits together in a harmonious system if you
> will only look at it in the illumination of the Gospel' . . . Our task
> with this world is not to explain it but to convert it . . . Christ
> said that the effect of his coming would be to set much at
> variance. We must expect the movement of his Spirit among us
> to produce sharper divisions as well as deeper unity.[10]

We take that warning seriously because, since Temple wrote
those words, we have seen and experienced the horrors of
modern war, with Hiroshima and Nagasaki, and the blatant and
horrific evils of the Holocaust. No gentle sense of working
towards harmony can by itself cut out such deep-seated infection from the body politic. In more recent times we have
observed the pain and cost of removing racial division and
hatred, for which there is no quick or easy solution. We saw that
in the life and death of Martin Luther King in the United States,
not least when some peaceable white pastors wrote to him in
prison asking him to stop his marches which so disturbed the
peace, and he replied crisply that 'peace is not the absence of
tension but the presence of justice'. Encountering division is not
cosy but costly: Martin Luther King paid dearly for his efforts
towards peace and harmony.

There is in the human condition not just the evil of division
which must be overcome, but there is a fundamental restlessness. Dietrich Bonhoeffer, who lost his life in the course of
the struggle within Germany, recognised the inevitability of
restlessness in humanity:

> It is a law of the world that there can never be rest and satisfac-
> tion here. Here no passion will ever be completely stilled. Every
> satisfaction has planted within itself that which drives beyond
> what has been achieved. The rich person wants to become richer,
> the mighty one mightier. The reason for this is that in the world
> there is never anything completely whole, so that each success,
> no matter how great, is only a partial success. If it is possible for
> there to be rest and silence anywhere, then it is only possible
> where there is wholeness, and that is only in God.[11]

We shall then recover wholeness fully only when God's work
is completed. It is only at the End that there will be fulfilment.
Recognising this ensures that we are temperate in our expec-
tations and have the humility to acknowledge that ultimately
wholeness is the gift of God, not the achievement of humanity.

The task before us then is large. But it is not impossible. The

Christian experience is that this work of reconciliation and integration can be achieved by inadequate people and muddled communities. In one of his Ordination Addresses the great Bishop of Durham, J. B. Lightfoot, reflected on the random group of early Christians to whom was entrusted the work of reconciliation:

> This little society of men and women; this motley group of Jews, Greeks, Syrians, immigrants from all parts of the world; mostly gathered together from the middle and lower classes of society, artisans and small shopkeepers where they were not slaves; poor, ill-educated, struggling for a livelihood; despised, where they were not ignored, by mighty Rome in the heart of which they lived; this little society, with its trials and its sufferings and its dissensions, is the kingdom of God, is the kingdom of heaven.[12]

It is not hard to see in Lightfoot's summary a reflection of the church today. For his ministry of reconciliation God chooses to use random groups who are at times pulling in different directions. He asks us to work for the unity of humanity in him, and we have to hold ourselves steady before God to see that vision of unity, allow the hands of God to grasp us, to let his spirit of unity work in and through us.

In the light of this deep sense of fragmentation and disintegration it is the purpose of this book to look again at the Christian traditions and see whether in yearning for coherence and wholeness we can in some measure rediscover the riches that God is giving to us. Only in doing God's work, and being in him, shall we find our ultimate fulfilment, cohesion and stillness. We shall look again at our understanding of God as Father and creator of us and of this one world. This will help us to come to terms with our earthiness and yet at the same time recognise that we are made in the image of God for work and companionship with him. We shall look at Jesus Christ as the Son of God who has engaged with this world, and transformed it. In doing that he has woven together God and humanity, and his work is to draw us all into himself. We shall also look at the Spirit of unity who enlivens God's world and his people within it. He is God at work in us raising us into the life of God himself. We shall try to draw these insights together by looking at the way in which that tripartite experience has been held together in the Christian understanding of the Trinity.

I hope to show that by giving our mind and understanding to God and what he has done and is doing, we shall find that we are being held together in him. Then I shall look also at how in prayer and sacrament we can realise this activity of God, and so more surely enter his integrated life. In the light of how we then perceive God's activity in the world there may be some illumination of how we should respond through Christian ministry in a divided world. Added as an appendix is the text of a sermon preached in 1995 which was in part the application of my main theme to a specific occasion. Throughout this brief review the primary recognition will be that we are held together in God.

Notes

1. Kenneth Stevenson, Enthronement sermon at Portsmouth, 16 December 1995, subsequently published in abbreviated form in the Portsmouth diocesan leaflet.
2. 1 Corinthians 9:22.
3. George Herbert, 'Giddinesse', stanzas 1 and 7, in *The Temple* (1633).
4. Quoted by Alec Vidler in 'The Limitations of William Temple', *Theology* (January 1976), p. 37.
5. Quoted in Martin Seymour Smith, *Hardy* (Bloomsbury, 1994), p. 332.
6. Ibid.
7. Leonard Hodgson, *The Doctrine of the Trinity* (Nisbet, 1943), p. 183f (italics mine).
8. Austin Farrer, *Reflective Faith*, edited by C. C. Conti (SPCK, 1972), p. 173.
9. For this, see for instance Jeremy Begbie in Hugh Montefiore (ed), *The Gospel and Contemporary Culture* (Mowbray, 1992), p. 58ff.
10. Quoted by Michael Ramsey, *From Gore to Temple* (Longmans, 1960), p. 160, but the source from Temple's writings is not given.
11. Dietrich Bonhoeffer, *Meditating on the Word* (Cowley, 1986), p. 62.
12. J. B. Lightfoot, *Ordination Addresses* (Macmillan, 1890), p. 208.

2

At One with the World

IF in the kitchen, the knife slips and you cut your finger it will bleed for a time, until the blood clots; then slowly the skin will grow again and there will be healing. So it is that a trivial domestic incident opens our eyes to a fundamental truth about ourselves. Our bodies have a natural, built-in power to heal themselves; we have an innate capacity to regain wholeness. Although there is disintegration and fragmentation in us and in this world of ours, there is also this innate, God-given tendency to heal and to regain wholeness. This acknowledged fact of self-healing in the body is matched by a natural self-healing in the mind, although as yet we are more reluctant to acknowledge that. When confronted by people with mental illness we have deliberately to recall for them and for ourselves this capacity for healing in our minds as well as in our bodies.

We can see this tendency to wholeness more strikingly when we observe so-called handicapped people. People who are blind often develop their other faculties to compensate: they become acute listeners, can identify people by their voices, detect the movement of traffic by ear. Deaf people often develop a sensitivity to vibration, so that a roomful of deaf people can be called to order by tapping on the floor. In commenting in such a way on so-called handicapped people we are of course observing ourselves. For we are all handicapped, although some handicaps show more obviously than others. A handicapped person with whom we live may be patently slow in movement; we by contrast are disturbingly quick in temper. He may have to search laboriously for words; we cannot stop ours from spilling out. So in observing and learning from the handicapped we are not from a vantage point of roundedness and wholeness commenting patronisingly on others who are impaired: we are allowing them to open our eyes to truths about ourselves.

So in a variety of ways we can see that human nature is always pushing towards wholeness. We shy away from this sometimes. If you sprain your ankle, and people sympathetically ask you how you are, you may reply, rather strangely, 'I am all right in myself; it's just my ankle.' But we cannot separate ourselves out quite so easily. There is an old Zulu proverb, 'When there is a thorn in the foot, the whole body has to stoop to pull it out.' As so often the African sees more clearly than the sophisticated Western European that we are more of an integrated whole than we often recognise.

If we are ill, well-meaning visitors may say to us, 'Never mind; time will heal.' But it is not time that heals: it is our human nature which heals itself – a process which indeed takes time. Nor is it the doctor or the drugs which heal. They may stave off and hold at bay the infection which is making us ill, or they may sort out the damage which has broken our normal pattern of fitness; but their actions are not so much healing in themselves as releasing the mind and the body to heal themselves. None of this removes or diminishes our dependence on time, on drugs or doctors, but it is to say that their role is secondary to our innate, God-given capacity to heal ourselves.

This sense of wholeness which we discover in ourselves is apparent also in the creation at large, although we often need help in discerning it. So much of our experience of the created world is fragmentary that often it takes the artists and poets to show us coherence. There is, for instance, an illuminating moment described in Peter Ackroyd's life of T. S. Eliot:

> He attended a performance of Stravinsky's *Le Sacre du Printemps* and at the end he stood up and cheered. Here . . . was an emblem for him of the way in which the complexities and even trivialities of contemporary existence, all that abruptness and dissonance which Stravinsky introduced into the texture of his music, could be rendered significant by an artistic vision which made use of the primeval drum beat.[1]

In our discordant world there is a hidden, deeper harmony which the artist draws out for us to sense and feel. For that matter artists help us to see people whole as well. The test of a good portrait is surely whether it depicts the person as a whole. It may not be able to portray the entire and total character but it must be more rounded than a photograph. A photo can only be a snapshot: a portrait takes a longer view. The camera is dead accurate, but that's the trouble: it will be *dead* accurate. A portrait is alive precisely because the artist has a capacity for seeing whole: he can portray a character rather than snap a person.

I

All this was seen in its own way by the writers of the creation stories in Genesis. The writers, ignorant of the niceties of evolution, make the point that God perceived the universe as an entity. In the Genesis story, the interrelatedness of existence is clear: God may have taken his time and needed a rest at the end, but he was making over a period one interlocking and interdependent universe. The creation stories see humanity taking its place in that universe: we cannot abstract ourselves from it. One of the creation narratives includes the firm statement, 'So God created man [in the sense of humanity as a whole] in his own image, in the image of God he created him, male and female he created them.'[2] So the ancient story puts us in our place as earthy creatures, and yet lifts us up to be colleagues and companions of God. To say we are in his image does not mean that we are in his shape, nor that we have his temperament. It means that humanity – not as it is, but as it is meant to be – bears the same character as God or is the stamp of God's very being. This is the insight given to us by the writer to the Hebrews as he contemplates the nature and reality of the true Man.[3]

One of the Genesis creation stories makes a further point about wholeness. God says 'It is not good that the man should be alone: I will make him a helper fit for him.'[4] The other story has the richer statement that God made man in his own image – male and female he created them. So in both creation accounts it is man and woman together who form a completed being. Argument today still swirls around whether men and women are equal. Many are convinced that they are equal; others are persuaded that men and women are both equal but men are more equal than women. Whatever the outcome of that continuing debate it is clear that man and woman are complementary: it is together that they constitute full humanity. They are not just 'partners' – the word now increasingly being used for close human relationships and so obscuring from us a truth we must recover. Surely the deeper insight is that men and women are not just partners; they make one another whole. There is a totality and completeness about the true man–woman relationship.

Our human wholeness then is to be seen in the context of our being an integral part of the material universe, in the context of marriage, and in the context of our relationship with God. But there are two further points to note before we leave the biblical insight into the nature of the created world. The first is the initiative of God. If we begin our observations of reality by trying to see ourselves in the perspective of eternity, the risk is that we shall inadvertently think that much if not all depends on us. Genesis states perceptively, 'In the beginning, God . . .'. St John begins his gospel in the same way: 'In the beginning was the Word . . .' Throughout, the Bible makes clear that everything is due to the initiative of God. The mere existence of this world is an expression of the outgoing generosity of God. It is his nature to give and to offer without first demanding response or responsibility. He made the world first and entrusted it to humanity afterwards. The initiative was and remains his.

The second biblical insight which we need to retain is that God's work of creation is not finished, and will not be so until the world itself ends. St John has Jesus saying 'My Father is working still, and I am working.'[5] That work of God was in one sense completed on the cross when Jesus in his last moments announced 'It is finished',[6] but St John also makes it clear that the completed work of Christ has to be made effective throughout the world by his disciples, when he records at the end of his gospel 'There are also many other things which Jesus did; were every one of them to be written, I suppose that the world itself could not contain the books that would be written.'[7] Clearly the implication is that we are the pages of those books: the hand of God continues to write his achievements on the parchment of human lives, and that inscribing will continue to the end of time. St Paul[8] sees the whole creation groaning and in anguish waiting for its completion and fulfilment: everything, it seems, is reaching out towards its creator, waiting to be completed.

This coherence of the universe and its reaching out towards God for its completion has been part of the vision of many Christian writers. One of the earliest was Tertullian who had a naïve and whimsical perception of creatures responding to their God:

> The whole creation prays. Cattle and wild beasts pray, and bend their knees, and in coming forth from their stalls and lairs look up to heaven, their mouths not idle, making the spirit move in their fashion. Moreover the birds taking flight lift themselves up to heaven and instead of hands, spread out the cross of their wings, while saying something which may be supposed to be a prayer.[9]

If then we are to understand ourselves and to live life as a whole in harmony with the world of which we are a part we have to be unashamed in acknowledging, and enjoying, our earthiness. Novelists have opened our eyes to see how people can be an integral part of their environment and as such wholly men of the earth. Thomas Hardy portrays Giles Winterborne in *The Woodlanders* as being the personification of the wood itself. He is described in the book by one of the other characters as able to 'speak in a tongue that nobody else knew . . . the tongue of the trees and fruits and flowers themselves'.[10] Hardy rather comically makes Giles look like walking nature:

> He looked and smelt like Autumn's very brother, his face being sunburnt to wheat-colour, his eyes blue as corn-flowers, his sleeves and leggings dyed with fruit-stains, his hands clammy with the sweet juice of apples, his hat sprinkled with pips, and everywhere about him that atmosphere of cider which at its first return each season has such an indescribable fascination for those who have been born and bred among the orchards.[11]

We sense that Giles can be at home and at ease with himself only in the context of the forest of which he is an integral part.

John Steinbeck, in *To a God Unknown*, set in southern California, has Joseph Wayne identifying himself with the earth both in its riches and its aridity. At the start of the novel Joseph, driven by a primitive urge, virtually marries the soil, almost trying to enter into the bosom of the earth. And at the end, when as a result of the failure of the rains the aridity of the earth dries Joseph out into a shrivelled person, he does not observe the barrenness of the earth so much as sense it within himself:

> For once he did not see the dry earth, cracked in long lightning lines. He did not feel the feeble tugging of the brittle brush as he rode through. His mind was a dusty road, and the weary cattle died in his brain.[12]

In a surprising and totally different context, this same sense of full-blooded earthiness was nicely caught by a young person in the course of an essay in a GCE exam:

> The disease that took her seemed too real for someone whose life had been as pale and timid as hers had been. She'd never really lived and yet she had to die.[13]

Surely our first human instinct should be to embrace this world and to sense our earthiness. Young people should be encouraged to affirm this world, to appreciate and enjoy it from the outset before they have necessarily to learn the puritan disciplines of avoiding its evils and abuses. Lady Violet Bonham Carter recalling her youth acknowledged her enthusiasm for life as she found it:

> Up went the curtain on the world. And what a world! I loved it at first sight – and plunged into it head foremost. There was no ice to break – the water was warm – and I was swimming.[14]

Undoubtedly young people need guidance; they need wisdom and experience to be passed on to them; they need to be taught and then to test out for themselves what is right and what is wrong. But this necessary discipline is to be grasped in the context of appreciating a rich and varied world which has been entrusted to us to enjoy and to pass to our successors.

In later years this acknowledgement of our earthiness includes the art of working with the grain of life rather than against it. Of course there is always the risk of being easygoing and merely opportunistic, but there is the need to have an eye to the general direction of life. Alistair Horne in his biography of Harold Macmillan quotes the Prime Minister as saying 'My belief is, when you get a chance, take it'[15] and goes on to recall Bismarck:

> A statesman has not to *make* history, but if ever in the events around him he hears the sweep of the mantle of God, then he must jump up and catch at its hem.

Of course this can be just trimming our sails to every passing puff of wind, but there is an art in discovering when that wind is the breath of God. And God's normal method of action is to work with the grain of the world. He is a master carpenter and has a deep respect for the material with which he is working: he works with it, not against it. In other words he does not normally suspend the regular laws of cause and effect but works with them. He suspends those laws or principles of life only on rare occasions: miracles are not cheap and common as plastic, but precious and rare as gold.

II

This unashamed working with the grain of the world and recognising our own earthiness is put in more Christian and spiritual terms by the seventeenth-century writer, Thomas Traherne:

> You never enjoy the world aright, till the sea itself floweth in your veins, till you are clothed with the heavens and crowned

with the stars . . . Till your spirit filleth the whole world, and the stars are your jewels; till you are familiar with the ways of God in all ages as with your walk and your table . . . till you delight in God for being good to all, you never enjoy the world . . . Yet further, you never enjoy the world aright, till you so love the beauty of enjoying it, that you are covetous and earnest to persuade others to enjoy it.[16]

Here is a deep acknowledgement of our earthiness, and an invitation to feel it, revel in it, and to be grateful for it. Traherne is sometimes criticised for being too positive about the world, and unaware of its evil and corruption, but in fact he has a sure sense of its being transformed by the intervention of God so that the world is once again what God intended it to be – the place for his kingdom. Surely Traherne is a sound tutor for an age which has largely lost the grace of gratitude. In more recent times Traherne's theme has been well expressed by Austin Farrer, who somewhere has written, 'The best way of thanking God is to taste his goodness with all our palate – enjoyment is the sincerest thanks.'

This sure acknowledgement of our earthiness which Traherne expresses as an Englishman is reflected in the observations of those of other nationalities. John V. Taylor recalls the insight of Africans to this aspect of our humanity. He records the astonishing answer of a Tswana to David Livingstone's question, 'What is holiness?':

When copious showers have descended during the night, and all the earth and leaves and cattle are washed clean and the sun rising shows a drop of dew on every blade of grass, and the air breathes fresh – that is holiness.

Many of the fathers of Eastern and Celtic monasticism might have said the same. So also would at least one of the great Jewish rabbinic schools.

A heathen asked Rabbi Joshua ben Karka, Why did God speak to Moses from the thorn bush? Rabbi Joshua replied, If he had spoken from a carob tree or from a sycamore you would have asked me the same question! But so as not to dismiss you without an answer, God spoke from the thorn bush to teach you that there is no place where the Shekinah is not, not even a thorn bush.[17]

The whole of this created world can speak to us of the things of God, for this earth bears his footprints, the hills speak of his glory, and the valleys echo with his words. Yet we often miss this through our capacity for taking so much for granted. There is an art in listening to the still small voice of God on this rugged earth. Thomas Merton tells how one New Year's day he took one of the two torn raincoats that hung in the grand parlour for the use of the monks and went out into the woods. He climbed.

> Bare woods and driving rain. There was a strong wind. When I reached the top I found there was something terrible about the landscape. But it was marvellous. The completely unfamiliar aspect of the forest beyond our rampart unnerved me. It was as though I were in another country . . . Halfway down, and in a place of comparative shelter, just before the pine trees begin, I found a bower God had prepared for me like Jonas's ivy. It had been designed especially for this moment. There was a tree stump, in an even place. It was dry and a small cedar arched over it, like a green tent, forming an alcove. There I sat in silence and loved the wind in the forest and listened for a good while to God.[18]

And to those who dare to write books or to work with words and their alluring delights he spoke out of his experience of a Trappist monastery:

> How weary I am of being a writer. How necessary it is for monks to work in the fields, in the rain, in the sun, in the mud, in the clay, in the wind: these are our spiritual directors and our novice-masters. They form our contemplation. They instil us with virtue. They make us as stable as the land we live in. You do not get that out of a typewriter.[19]

The danger of this full blooded appreciation of the natural world of which we are part is that we can take Nature itself to be God, or too naïvely think that we are nearer to God's heart in a garden than anywhere else on earth. There is currently renewed interest in the natural world symbolised by the popularity of television programmes about wild life. Environmentalists have lifted our awareness of our surroundings and enlarged our sense of responsibility. Animal rights organisations have made us more sensitive to the wonders and delights of other creatures. All this is great gain and consistent with the Christian understanding of creation as entrusted to humanity for treasuring. But in some of this expansion of concern for the world around us there is a failure to see the ruthless cruelty of the animal kingdom – nature red in tooth and claw. We cannot idealise, still less idolise, Nature, and ignore its vicious streak. Thomas Hardy in *The Woodlanders* portrays sombrely the twistedness of nature at the time that Giles Winterborne is dying in a hut in the forest:

> . . . trees close together, wrestling for existence, their branches disfigured with wounds resulting from their mutual rubbings and blows . . . Beneath them were the rotting stumps of those of the group that had been vanquished long ago, rising from their mossy setting like black teeth from green gums.[20]

While we are right to immerse ourselves in the material and animal world, we also have to stand back and use our critical faculties: we have to be detached from the world as well as to be immersed in it.

III

A sound appreciation of the natural world moves us from a full recognition of our earthiness and our material humanity to a sense of detachment and an acknowledgement of God the creator. Here Julian of Norwich is a sure guide. She is best known for her comment about the world being as a hazelnut in the palm of her hand, but this well-known vision of Julian's needs to be seen in context.

> He showed me more, a little thing, the size of a hazelnut, on the palm of my hand, round like a ball. I looked at it thoughtfully and wondered, 'What is this?' And the answer came, 'It is all that is made'. I marvelled that it continued to exist and did not suddenly disintegrate; it was so small. And again my mind supplied the answer, 'It exists, both now and for ever, because God loves it'. In short everything owes its existence to the love of God.

No sooner has Julian delighted in the richness and goodness of creation than she stands back from it.

> We have got to realise the littleness of creation and to see it for the nothing that it is before we can love and possess God who is uncreated.[21]

Three chapters later she explains that creation is as nothing in comparison with God:

> I was well aware that the universe is great and huge, beautiful and good, but the reason why it seemed so small was that I saw it in the presence of him who is its Creator: and to a soul who sees the Creator of all everything seems insignificant.[22]

So Julian moves from the fullest recognition of the riches of creation to see that totality in perspective: she sees through the world to the Creator beyond. She holds God's immanence in the world and his transcendence beyond it in perfect harmony. It is often those who have detached themselves from the world and entered the religious life who have the surest sense of the treasures and riches of this earth. Evelyn Underhill once observed that if we want to find the person who combines spiritual passion with appreciation of a good cup of coffee we should go to a convent.[23] It is perhaps those who have renounced the world who treasure it most profoundly.

This understanding of God as creator and sustainer of the universe is of course known as the doctrine of God the Creator or the doctrine of creation. Doctrines are not cold statements of the mind but warm statements of experience. A doctrine has inescapably to be hammered out and burnished in the forge of academic theology, but the wrought-iron work which is still being shaped and polished there is not an ornament for the studies of the scholars but a working symbol for the living church. Doctrines are not the possession of the professional theologians but the accumulated experience of the working and praying church. Austin Farrer once wrote that no dogma deserves its place unless it is prayable, and no Christian deserves his dogma who does not pray them.[24] So the doctrine of God as creator is not just an intellectual or academic definition but a statement about experience, attitudes and relationships. God as creator is Father and we are his dependent children whom he is loving into holiness as he encourages us to stretch ourselves to realise our gifts, to come to terms with our limitations and our potential and so to grow into a mature relationship with him. He has no interest in keeping us as perpetual children: he is a better educator than that. He wants us to be partners in his continuing life and activity.

For that we need first to be open to the reality and mystery of his being and not to domesticate him to human concepts and words, although in part that is inescapable as we try to speak and write of our experience of him. Goethe once said that it was our duty to fathom what can be fathomed and to bow in reverence before the unfathomable. And St Hilary warned us

We are compelled to attempt what is unattainable, to climb where we cannot reach, to speak what we cannot utter. Instead of the bare adoration of faith we are compelled to entrust the deep things of religion to the perils of human expression.[25]

That is what we are now daring to do, and it is right that we should use words to try to describe our experience of the living God, for it is often through words that inspiration and enlightenment reach us. Yet in using words we have to recognise that the truth and the mystery of God lie beyond the words.

Second, we need above all to be grateful to God for what he has given and still gives us. The Christian church has spoken and written much of the failures of human beings. There can be no denying that fact of life. Yet more important than human failure is the graciousness of God. We should be giving more time to gratitude to God than to deploring our weakness. Gratitude to God is at the heart of Christian worship, although in practice often obscured by other words and actions, and a renewed discipline of gratitude to God might do more to enliven the church than a mass of other programmes and policies. William Law, a seventeenth-century English divine, once wrote:

> Would you know who is the greatest saint in the world? It is not he who prays most, or fasts most, it is not he who gives most alms, or is most eminent for temperance, chastity or justice. But it is he who is always thankful to God . . . and who has a heart always ready to praise God . . . This is the perfection of all virtues . . . Joy in God and thankfulness to God is the highest perfection of a divine and holy life . . . To thank God only for such things as you like is no more a proper act of piety than to believe only what you see is an act of faith.[26]

Because wholeness in humanity and in the universe is God-given, it will not be complete until we and the universe find our unity in God who gives it. We have already seen that this is part of St Paul's vision where he writes of the whole creation groaning and travailing together waiting for its fulfilment.[27] And we are aware that we experience true integrity only when we dedicate ourselves to God and enter into him. Much of Christian spirituality centres on this unitive way – on offering ourselves to God, responding to his creative power so that we may discover sure integration with him: that we may evermore dwell in him and he in us. Our integrity is complete only as we yield ourselves to him.

This wholeness has been given to us by God, but we have to recognise it, appropriate it, and allow others to enter it. In our tradition of spirituality there are repeated expressions of this aspiration for unity with God. Perhaps the best known is the prayer of St Augustine of Hippo:

Lord, take my heart from me for I cannot give it thee; keep it for thyself for I cannot keep it for thee; and save me in spite of myself.

There is the prayer of St Ignatius Loyola:

Take, Lord, all my liberty. Receive my memory, my understanding and my whole will. Whatsoever I have and possess thou hast given to me. To thee I restore it wholly, and to thy will I utterly surrender it for thy direction. Give me the love of thee only and I am rich enough. Nor ask I anything beside.

In more recent times there is Dag Hammarskjöld:

Each morning we must hold out the chalice of our being to receive, to carry, and to give back. It must be held out empty – for the past must be reflected only in its polish, its shape, its capacity; and those things which for our unworthiness we dare not, and for our blindness we cannot ask, vouchsafe to give us.[28]

This unitive approach moves perhaps even deeper in the prayer of Julian of Norwich which comes close to her passage about the hazelnut:

God, of your goodness give me yourself, for you are sufficient for me. I cannot properly ask anything less, to be worthy of you. If I were to ask less, I should always be in want. In you alone do I have all.[29]

This rich tradition of spirituality centring in dedication and desire for unity with God is rooted in the writing of St Paul. In his letter to the Romans[30] he has a fine sentence, 'I appeal to you therefore, brethren, by the mercies of God to present your bodies as a living sacrifice.' The context is significant, and we note the key word 'therefore'. In some contexts this can be just a link word meaning no more than 'now' or 'then', but in this paragraph it is surely a controlling word. St Paul has been writing about the providential activity of God as he steers his way through the chaos of the world to achieve his aim. This one word 'therefore' here marks the turning-point from doctrine (in the first eleven chapters of his letter) to ethics (from chapter twelve onwards), from the action of God to the response expected from humanity. St Paul draws attention to the actions of God and so to the divine initiative, and *therefore* invites his readers to offer themselves to God in response as a living sacrifice.

Here then is a way in which we can follow the spiritual

masters of the past centuries and begin to enter a deep and rich unity which overcomes the fragmentation of so much of life as we experience it from day to day. A sure recognition of our earthiness does not leave us earthbound, but acknowledges that we are the creatures of God who offers us union with him. The way is not easy but it is a sure path to integrity and coherence.

Notes

1. Peter Ackroyd, *T. S. Eliot* (Sphere, 1988), p. 112.
2. Genesis 1:27.
3. Hebrews 1:3.
4. Genesis 2:18.
5. John 5:17.
6. John 19:30.
7. John 21:25.
8. Romans 8:22.
9. Tertullian, *On the Prayer*, chapter 29 (translation in E. Evans (ed and trans), *Tertullian's Tract on the Prayer* (SPCK, 1953)).
10. Thomas Hardy, *The Woodlanders* (1887), chapter 44.
11. Ibid., chapter 28.
12. John Steinbeck, *To a God Unknown* (Heinemann, 1933), chapter 24.
13. Quoted in *The Times*, 19 August 1980.
14. *The Listener* (28 June 1956), quoted by Alec Vidler, *Essays in Liberality* (SCM, 1957), p. 108.
15. Alistair Horne, *Macmillan*, Volume 1 (Macmillan, 1988), p. 454.
16. Thomas Traherne (c. 1636–1674), *Centuries* (first published in 1908), I, 29, 30, 31.
17. John V. Taylor, *The Primal Vision* (SCM Press, 1963), p. 201f, quoting from David Livingstone, *Expedition to the Zambesi* (1865), p. 64, and C. G. Montefiore and H. Loewe, *A Rabbinic Anthology* (Macmillan, 1938), p. 13.
18. Thomas Merton, *The Sign of Jonas* (Harcourt Brace, 1953), p. 263f.
19. Ibid., p. 321.
20. Thomas Hardy, *The Woodlanders*, chapter 42.
21. Julian of Norwich, *Revelations of Divine Love*, chapter 5.
22. *Revelations of Divine Love*, chapter 8.
23. Charles Williams (ed), *The Letters of Evelyn Underhill* (Longmans, Green and Co., 1943), p. 78.
24. Austin Farrer, *Lord I Believe* (Church Union, 1955), p. 8.
25. Quoted Robert Runcie, *One Light for One World* (SPCK, 1988), p. 64.

26. William Law, *A Serious Call to a Devout and Holy Life* (1728), chapter 15.
27. Romans 8:22.
28. Dag Hammarskjöld, *Markings* (ET Faber and Faber, 1964), p. 127.
29. Julian of Norwich, *Revelations of Divine Love*, chapter 5.
30. Romans 12:1.

3

The Man of Integrity

AS I face life with its multiple and distracting pressures and demands, I look for some way through. I hope for some person who has engaged with the fragmentariness of life, who has experienced the shards of pain which unexpectedly stab me as I find so much that fractures in my hands, and yet who retains and achieves integrity. I need someone who has grappled with all that I have to face and yet has held together.

The Christian conviction is that in the life of Christ we see God himself taking this uncertain human life with both hands, making sense of it, living it with integrity, and in so doing, filling it with a new vitality which is coherent. Even if we read the gospels as no more than pieces of ancient literature, we can sense the fragmentary nature of existence and the increasingly clear conviction that Jesus held it whole and together. The earliest of the gospels, St Mark's, is written throughout in clipped sentences, and even when he moves into the more continuous passion narrative, the sentences are sharp and staccato. His literary style, quite apart from the content of his gospel, conveys the stabbing pain and the piercing anguish.

The earlier part of Mark's gospel is episodic, consisting of a number of incidents and events; they seem like separate pearls being strung together to give form and pattern. It is as though the writer is making a literary patchwork quilt, using separate pieces of material of different colours and designs, and stitching them together into a pattern which yet leaves exposed the independent constituent parts. The later gospel writers in their different ways smooth this out, giving us a rounder picture, and eventually in the latest of the gospels, St John's, Jesus becomes a poised and commanding figure who, although at the mercy of human beings and relentlessly handed over to the powers that be, yet is totally in command, holding everything in the palm of his hand. Taken as a group, the gospels, just by their style and pattern, move us from an awareness of the fragmentary to a vision of a total person, the true man of integrity.

More significant than the literary style of the gospels is their content. The portrayal of Jesus in the gospel narratives makes it clear that Jesus engages with all the uncertainties of human existence and pulls them together. John Barton has put the point for us well:

> To live a human life means not to know for certain what each day will bring, still less what the end of it all will be. But the human vocation is to live through all these unpredictabilities with a consistent purpose and a consistent character, and that vocation Jesus, as we see him in the gospels, embraced to the full . . . God's involvement with human life in Jesus is an acceptance of all this arbitrariness, not an act which sweeps it away and replaces it with a grand design leaving no room for error.[1]

John Barton goes on to draw on Russell Harty's way of dividing humanity into radiators and drains. Jesus was not a drain, drawing to himself the dross and rubbish of life, so much as a radiator, warming up every person and situation he touched. He came not to decry human life or play it down; he came to grasp life, and fill it to overflowing.

I

Jesus was a joiner. The gospels make little of the fact. Mark includes it as a casual remark from local people. Matthew, almost as though he were embarrassed by the fact, alters this piece of casual local gossip and puts the information at one generation's remove: 'Is not this the carpenter's *son*?' Luke and John ignore the point altogether. So does St Paul unless he has this in mind when he refers to Christ taking the form of a slave – the ordinary artisan in an ancient society. In any case the word used by Mark and Matthew need not mean carpenter: it indicates any handyman or craftsman. It is tradition rather than reliable knowledge that has taken the word to mean carpenter. Yet there is no cause for challenging that tradition, and by using the contemporary word 'joiner' rather than carpenter other understandings open up.

Jesus was not a loner. When he set about his life's work, as distinct from any paid employment, he worked closely with friends and colleagues, and among them he appears to have had three who were close associates. At times he had to give his energies to getting his team to work creatively together, and he tried to curb rivalry between them. Beyond that, he was ready to speak with crowds when they collected. Although he chose moments when he withdrew and was alone (nearly always to pray), these times appear to be periods which were not isolating as though he wanted to get away from his work of pulling people together; they were periods which undergirded his work of drawing people to himself and to one another.

Jesus was not just a social worker. He was a joiner in the profoundest sense. If indeed he worked with wood, then no doubt he joined together different pieces, so that separate bits came together, moved together, breathed together. But it was not just wood that he joined. In his very being Jesus brought together time and eternity, heaven and earth. The gospels make it clear that his life's work was to be a joiner of God and humanity, working them so that they moved and breathed together. That was meat and drink to him: St John records Christ as saying, 'My food is to do the will of him that sent me, and to accomplish his work.'[2] His daily work may have been to join together wood; his life's work was to join together God and humanity.

St John in his gospel pulls together these two senses of Jesus being a joiner when he records Christ as saying that when he is lifted up on the cross he will draw all people to himself.[3] At the moment when his life's work reaches its climax and fulfilment, and his integration of God and humanity reaches its crucial conclusion, he draws all humanity together to himself.

If we look at the work of Christ in more traditional and theological terms we note that the catholic tends to stress the primary significance of the incarnation, and sees the atonement as the inevitable consequence and working out of the incarnation. The protestant sees Christ's primary work as atonement, and the incarnation as a necessary preliminary to that. Both are right, and surely we need to see the wholeness of Christ's life and work together and not strive to separate out the constituent parts. Jesus was the human embodiment of God. The person and being of Christ brought into harmony and unity the human and the divine. What he was in himself he worked out in his life and work. What he said, and the way he taught, show how his mind brought heaven and earth together. The cross marks the place where the human and the divine intersected in action. There on Calvary was hammered out and marked for all time the meeting place of God and humanity.

So the crucifixion expressed, achieved and completed in action what Christ already was in his person. As Dinsmore wrote, 'There was a cross in the heart of God before there was one planted on the green hill outside Jerusalem.'[4] There can be no denying that the crucifixion was an act of reconciliation, a drawing together of God and humanity. The resurrection was an even further expression of this unity of the human and the divine. In the raising of Jesus from the dead, God drew together all the parts and pieces of the life of Jesus and recreated them into a united being who transcends time and death. We see then that in Jesus' birth, his being, his death, his resurrection – in every aspect of his life and work – he draws all together.

This drawing together of all things in Christ is seen by poets and writers with a vibrancy of word and image that quickens our perception. Take for instance T. S. Eliot:

> But to apprehend
> The point of intersection of the timeless
> With time, is an occupation for the saint –
> No occupation either, but something given
> And taken, in a lifetime's death in love . . .
> These are only hints and guesses,
> Hints followed by guesses; and the rest
> Is prayer, observance, discipline, thought and action.
> The hint half guessed, the gift half understood is
> Incarnation.[5]

Another perception comes from Christopher Nolan, who won the Irish Spastics Society Literary Prize, and who writes movingly out of his experience of being paralysed from the neck down. He has to speak with his eyes. Because of this heavy handicap he hammers out his words laboriously and as a result packs them with meaning, writing in a style which combines poetry and prose. He writes about himself in the third person, seeing himself as Joseph Meehan:

> He [the reference is to Nolan himself] attempted to rescue crippled man from pits of oblivion and set about shattering the sacred-held image of handicap as being godsent. Assessing the old beliefs, he found them cruelly wanting. He voiced his doubts about God being bothered about spastics; rather he set about giving credit where credit was due. Restfully reassured by his new friends, Joseph now nominated God in a new light: 'Man is God hesitant and God is Man hesitantly trying to help.'[6]

At first sight that is not orthodox theology, but is this not Nolan, from deep inside the experience of severe handicap, finding his way to the interpenetration of the human and the divine? God is Man, through Gethsemane and the passion, through handicap with all its limitations, entering deep and whole into the confines of the human condition. Humanity in response aspires to the divine life but hesitates in awe and trembling before daring to be drawn into the transcendent life of God.

II

This work of integrating time and eternity, God and humanity, was achieved by the Logos or Word of God and was articulated in the words of Christ. We find in the parables of Jesus not just vivid illustrations of divine truth but an insight into the way to perceive that truth. The manner of Jesus' teaching is as instructive as the matter. Some of the parables appear to be well-known yarns told in the village gossip sessions, which Jesus retells, but giving them a new twist. For instance, he takes the old story of Dives and Lazarus and tells it again with a new ending which transforms and enlivens it. Other parables are snapshots of everyday life held up like old colour transparencies to the light of God so that his glory shines through and we see life in its true and divine colours. Jesus sees God through the everyday scenes of farmers at work, wedding receptions, the labour market, the treatment of promiscuous adolescents. These everyday events and common stories are the lens through which he perceives the eternal and the divine activity.

Sometimes we obscure from ourselves the meaning of the parables by turning them back to front. We tend to turn them round and focus overmuch on what they tell us about ourselves rather than what they say about God. When Jesus wanted to give us a picture of a loving, yearning God whose heart runs out to us even when we abandon him and revel in the merely earthy and the secular, he told the story that we now call the Prodigal Son. That name is strange. Surely the parable was primarily about the Generous Father rather than about the self-indulgent son.

Or when Jesus wanted to demonstrate that God cares dispassionately and compassionately for all, he tells the parable that we call the Labourers in the Vineyard. But his primary purpose was surely to focus not on the labourers and their unequal rates of pay, but on God and his all-embracing concern for each and every person, not least the lower or less attractive in society. By the way we label Jesus' parables we turn them round and make them about us rather than about God. A truer evaluation of the purpose of the parables is surely that Jesus, by this brilliant and evocative method of teaching, opens our eyes to the truth of God through getting us to look afresh at the everyday reality before our eyes. He draws heaven and earth together.

Then in the pages of the gospels we see how much of his teaching is in the form of extravagant and perceptive seeds of truth which have to be rooted in the stony ground around our homes. The gospels give us uncut gems of divine wisdom in the Sermon on the Mount and we see them being ground and polished by abrasive, harsh reality. Jesus said, 'If anyone strikes you on the right cheek, turn to him the other also.'[7] When precisely that happened to Jesus he may have turned his face, but only to speak with judgement and challenge.

> When he said this, one of the officers standing by struck Jesus with his hand, saying, 'Is that how you answer the high priest?' Jesus answered him, 'If I have spoken wrongly, bear witness to the wrong; but if I have spoken rightly, why do you strike me?'[8]

So the seeds of divine truth root and grow in the rough earth of circumstance. If we are to be grasped by the full strength of Jesus' words, we have to watch for how they move into action even in the pages of the New Testament itself.

The way Jesus told stories, and the way he taught and put that teaching into practice, are themselves expressions of how he held together in himself the human and the divine. He integrated the firmness and permanence of the divine with the fragmentary and uncertainty of the human.

One of the striking facts about the way the earliest Christians spoke about Jesus was the way they saw him as a corporate or inclusive personality.[9] Those who lived and worked with him clearly knew him as an individual person, but from early days they found they could do justice to their experience of him as an individual only if they spoke of living in and through him as though he summarised in himself all that they aspired to. The earliest of the Christian writers, St Paul, wrote often of the Christian experience of being 'in Christ', although he was more cautious in writing about Christ being in us. And he understood this not so much as an individual experience but rather of all Christian believers being joined together to live corporately in Christ. The authors of the gospels expressed this in slightly different terms: they were ready to identify Christ with those who believed in him. Matthew, for instance, has Jesus saying, 'As you did it to one of the least of these my brethren, you did it to me.'[10] St Luke, in Acts, identifies Jesus with his followers in the striking statement at Paul's conversion, 'Saul, Saul, why do you persecute me?'[11] St John has a more individual understanding than St Paul of the interpenetration of Christ and each of his followers, and is willing to speak equally of Christ in us and of ourselves in Christ. Whatever the differences in detail, the New Testament writers give clear expression to this striking perception that we are integrated into Christ. Undoubtedly Christ calls us to be his followers and sets a pattern for living which we can imitate, but justice is not done to our understanding of him until we see ourselves as being drawn individually and together into the very life of Christ.

This idea of a corporate personality may strike some as strange. Yet we find it in different forms in contemporary life. In her moving account of her struggle to achieve peace and justice for the Palestinian people, Hanan Ashrawi describes how she approached Nelson Mandela because he seemed to be not just another politician in a foreign land working for the liberation of his people, but a man of stature who belongs to all. She wrote to Mandela:

> Teach us the secret of your calm, of your dignity and your power, so that we too may share the glory of the moment . . . We have been sadly diminished, but we too can lay claim to you, for you do not belong to only one race or one nation. The whole world has taken comfort and inspiration from your stature and guidance, and we in particular need you . . . Your triumph is ours as well, but we still need to take on your patience and your wisdom.[12]

Here is a contemporary picture of how a man who has borne suffering without bitterness and has risen above so much disintegrating and destructive human behaviour appears to be a person to whom others want to lay claim. Even more strikingly than this, the early Christians saw Christ as a man who transcends the limitations and divisions of race, nation, time and space, and perceived him as a person who incorporates all within himself. Nothing less than this perception does justice to the impact Christ made on his contemporaries, and on those who since then have been drawn by his magnetic power.

III

Let us now turn to the final moments of Jesus' life and see the compelling integrity of the cross and the empty tomb. There is no doubt that in the gospels the heart and centre of the life and work of Christ is his death and resurrection. The passion narratives, particularly in Mark and Matthew, dominate the whole gospel: here, on the cross, is worked out in dramatic terms the whole meaning and purpose of the work of God. Austin Farrer provides us with an effective starting point from which to consider this crucial point in the life of Christ:

> The centre and seal of revelation is Jesus Christ alone. The significance of Genesis is, that it contains the picture of an idea which Christ proved by living it out. For it is not simply that Jesus saw the handiwork of God in lilies, and his providence in the fall of a sparrow. It is that he wagered his life on creative power. Who can raise the dead? No one: in the literal sense, not God himself. The dead are not raised: immortalised men are not galvanised corpses. What is called the resurrection of the dead is a remaking of their life, in a stuff and in a fashion which are known to God alone. If we are made, we can be remade: he who created can create anew. Jesus Christ experimented with creation when he threw himself and all the world's hopes into nothingness, by the death of the cross.[13]

Farrer here shows how in looking at the cross we are not looking at an isolated event or doctrine, but at the whole activity of God through a chosen lens. The crucifixion becomes the means through which we have a clearer vision of creation and rec-reation, or resurrection.

Over the centuries Christian thinkers have gazed at the cross, studied it, written about it, depicted it in art, and struggled to plumb its depth. They have come up with theories. There are differing theories and explanations even in the New Testament itself about how and why the cross is so effective. Much depends on what writers see as the deepest threat to human existence. If you see demon possession as the greatest threat to human life then the redeemer will be the person who overpowers the demons. If you think of slavery as the greatest threat to human life, then the deliverer will be the person who brings slavery to an end. If, with Athanasius, you think death is the harshest threat to human life, then the saviour will be the person who overcomes death. If, with Anselm, you think inability to make adequate recompense for the wrongs done as the heaviest threat, then the redeemer will be the person who bears the punishment that should be ours. If, with Hodgson, you think that human hatred is the venom which threatens human life, then the saviour will be the Red Cross man who sucks the poison out of the world's system.

Sometimes people pick on one or other of these explanations and try to make it the sole interpretation of the cross. The church throughout its history has steadily refused to be narrow or constrictive here. It sees rather the need of all these pictures to work together in harmony to give a composite understanding of why and how the cross reconciles God and humanity. Our job is to work through these explanations, derive insight and wisdom from them, and then just kneel before the cross and see and experience the drawing together of God and humanity.

Whatever else these theories of atonement may be saying to us, the least they present to our minds is that God forgives and calls on us to be the forgiving people. God does not wait for people to come scurrying back from their self-centred escapades, or to drop to their knees in penitence before his arms are open in welcome. God forgives without waiting and without bargaining. As John V. Taylor has written,

> Forgiveness has to be premature or it is not forgiveness. Grace cannot wait and see. It acts as though the relationship were already made good, even before that has happened.[14]

God draws humanity back to himself with open arms – arms nailed open by divine love for all time. The cross is the moment of reconciliation, and St Paul reminded the congregation in Corinth that they were charged with making this reconciliation known not only by what they said but also by what they did.[15]

Forgiveness is not elbowing aside an offender and announcing a blanket amnesty. Nor is it trying or pretending to forget: deep inner wounds remain and cannot be ignored or forgotten. Forgiveness is facing the memory of the offence and refusing to allow that memory to damage present or future relationship. Forgiveness, one of the supreme gifts of God, has to be in, and be evident in, the life and work of the individual, the church and of society.

Dag Hammarskjöld wrote:

> Forgiveness breaks the chain of causality because he who 'forgives' you – out of love – takes upon himself the consequences of what *you* have done. Forgiveness, therefore, always entails a sacrifice. The price you must pay for your own liberation through another's sacrifice, is that you in turn must be willing to liberate in the same way, irrespective of the consequence to yourself.[16]

A particular instance of the grace of forgiveness was evident in the life of the church in northern Nigeria in 1987. During the course of one weekend, of the 119 Christian churches in Zaria 116 were set on fire. This was the work of Muslim extremists. Not content with firing the churches, they then went to the homes of prominent Christians, poured petrol over their pets and domestic animals and set fire to them and then to their houses. The dismay and anger this caused is not hard to imagine. I was able to visit the church in Nigeria not many months after these tragic events. As they showed me the charred ruins of their houses and churches, the memory that remains convincingly with me is that those treated in this way recalled the continuing anguish, but they bore no malice. They told me how immediately this arson had happened their bishop came to see them and reminded them that revenge, though the normal human reaction to such treatment, was not the Christian way. They were to bear this suffering in their hearts and carry no ill will. These people unquestionably felt the pain and anguish of this experience for months afterwards, but the quiet and courageous way in which they could speak of what had happened to them was remarkable evidence of the redeeming power of forgiveness, and I remain lastingly grateful for this compelling witness to Christian grace.

The integrity of Christ and of his work of integration is further illuminated in a striking incident recorded by Emmi Bonhoeffer in her account of the Auschwitz trials. She found herself ashamed of the way in which some of the defendants claimed as an excuse for their deeds that atrocities had been committed by others. In desperation, those on trial referred to Dresden, to Hiroshima, and to the Russian Tscheka massacre. As she listened to the trials of her fellow-Germans and to this attempt at defence she could say only that the dirt of others can never be the soap with which we clean ourselves. She then records the evidence of one of the witnesses who had been in a concentration camp:

A large number of women with small children are told to strip before the so called 'shower rooms'. One mother, carrying a maybe one-year-old, until now gullible enough that she simply could not let herself believe the rumours that circulated about the camp, suddenly sees what is to happen. Gripped by despair, she throws herself down at the feet of a young guard imploring him to save at least her child. And she reminds him that he surely has wife and child himself and that he therefore must have mercy. What shall he do? He pushes her aside and shoves her forward with the others, across the threshold and inside. But at the moment when the doors are closing, screaming, My Wife, My Child, he thrusts himself into the throng and dies with them there in the gas.[17]

Here is not just a moving illustration of how one man can identify with suffering humanity through, so to speak, incarnation and sacrifice, but an indication of how the contemporary world illuminates and deepens our understanding of God and of Christ.

IV

The resurrection is also a work of integration. Harry Williams gives a telling picture of the integrating work of resurrection.

If we may put it so without irreverence, the ministry of Jesus from the earthly point of view appears to have been a matter of odds and ends. When finally he went to the cross, what, in terms of human achievement, had Jesus done? He had preached to the multitudes – they had listened, wondered and gone away. He had healed a considerable number of the sick – but where did they disappear to? . . . He had fed the multitude in the wilderness – we are told explicitly that they failed to understand what he did. He made a rich young man think – we are not told with what result, except that the young man went away sorrowful. He had rescued a prostitute. He had chosen and trained twelve special friends – of these, in the hour of crisis, the most intelligent betrayed him, the most affectionate denied him. He had had half an hour's interesting conversation with a Roman civil servant. He had comforted a dying scoundrel. Sent into the world to rescue the millions of mankind, to bring the whole earth back to God, his work in the end amounted to a number of separated bits and pieces – each thing in itself of course worthwhile, but without any apparent cohesion, a number of individual works performed on a number of different days in a number of different places, scattered and divided by time and distance, without any perfection of wholeness or integration. But in the resurrection of Jesus, God took these bits and pieces of a disjointed ministry and wove from them a single garment of salvation for the whole world. The many and various things which Jesus did in Galilee and Judaea were not lost. They were raised with him on the first Easter morning.[18]

This insight can be put alongside the experience of being at the bedside of a dying person. As I contemplate the frail shell of

a person struggling for breath and barely aware of the sur-
rounding world, I wonder where the 'person' now is. The human
being I have known is not just the physical frame at this point
reaching its end, but the totality that this person has been
throughout his or her life. Even when this person was in full
vigour at any one time, I encountered only a cross-section of the
total being. A person ultimately surely must be everything that
he has been at varying moments throughout his life. What God
seems to have done at the resurrection on the first Easter Sunday
was to take all the bits and pieces of the life of Christ, and
recreated them into a totality which transcends time and space.
So the Risen Christ retained the marks that life had made on
him – the marks of the nails and spear, but also the wounds and
scars of misunderstanding and desertion – but now all that he
had been made by the events and encounters of his whole life
was recreated into a new life which summarised all that he had
been and still was. That recreated, re-integrated life transcends
the limitations of time and space, as the gospel writers in their
own idiom convincingly portray.

It is into that resurrection of Christ that we are drawn and we
are part of him. In one sense we have contributed to the making
of Jesus by being who and what we are. No one of us is an
isolated individual, created out of the blue, and untrammelled
by engagement with others. On the contrary we are who and
what we are as a result of our encounters with other people.
Parents, teachers, friends, colleagues, critics have all in their
several ways shaped and made us: that is what it is to be human.
And because Jesus also is human, he too was shaped and
moulded in part by the impact of others on him. Christ is a
corporate personality with whom we are engaged, and into
whom we are drawn, not least in resurrection. Austin Farrer has
put it strikingly:

> Have you reflected that Jesus was that Jesus because of Mary and
> Joseph and the village rabbi, a man to us unknown; above all
> because of the disciples to whom he gave himself and the poor
> people to whose need he ministered? But for these people, he
> would have been another Jesus. To be a man, he must have them,
> and to continue a man (as he still indeed is) he must retain
> them. So the life of God, incarnate in Jesus, cannot be locked
> within his breast; it becomes a spreading complex of personal
> being, centred in Jesus, and annexing his companions. Though
> we are each but a minute cell in the social body of Christ, yet,

taking us in the lump and in the gross, he is what he humanly is by his relation to us.[19]

Resurrection is not resuscitation. When there has been death, we can never go back. Only new life is possible. Resurrection is a wholly new act of creation by God using the raw material of what a person has been and is. We see that displayed on Easter day, although it stretches our minds beyond the everyday and remains a mystery. We experience that same resurrection in small and modest ways from time to time as we become aware of God pulling us together, rolling away the rocklike obstinacy of our set and settled minds and raising us to new perceptions, new hopes, new life. There is a graceful picture of this almost hidden resurrection in George Eliot's *Silas Marner*. The weaver has been hoarding his gold and stowing it under the floor boards, and where his treasure is, there is his heart also. When the gold is stolen, his world as he knew it comes to an end. Then, totally unexpectedly, he meets a young girl of golden hair who lifts him to a new vision, a new sense of values, a new life:

> The disposition to hoard had been utterly crushed at the very first by the loss of his long-stored gold: the coins he earned afterwards seemed as irrelevant as stones brought to complete a house suddenly buried by an earthquake . . . And now something had come to replace his board which gave a growing purpose to the earnings, drawing his hope and joy continually onward beyond the money. In old days there were angels who came and took men by the hand and led them away from the city of destruction. We see no white-winged angels now. But yet men are led away from threatening destruction: a hand is put into theirs, which leads them forth gently towards a calm and bright land, so that they look no more backward; and the hand may be a little child's.[20]

Some will have had experience of grave illness striking without warning in a family, so that life is shattered. There may be full recovery, but grave illness can leave people damaged or handicapped. This partial or miniature death can be met either by cold resignation or by a steady recognition that the resurrection power of God can work to create new life not just at the end of time but now and here in circumstances and ways we had not envisaged. It is open to all of us, however limiting our circumstance, to begin to enter into the resurrection of Christ.

V

A brief review of parables that Jesus told, and of his life, death and resurrection, opens our eyes to see that here is a man into whose life and experience we are drawn, partly because of his magnetic and compelling appeal, but more surely because we see that his secret lies in holding God and humanity together. The entire life and work of Christ is to draw people together and into himself. By responding to that act of God our broken and fragmented lives can find a new coherence. Seeing Christ as holding everything in himself and drawing us all to him is expressed firmly in the later letters of St Paul. God, he writes, has 'set forth in Christ as a plan for the fullness of time, to unite all things in him, things in heaven and things on earth'.[21] And in more rounded terms he makes the same point at the start of another letter where he writes that Christ 'is before all things and in him all things hold together'.[22] It is that insight that surely provides us with the integrity for which we seek and yearn.

Notes

1. John Barton, *Love Unknown* (SPCK, 1990), p. 15.
2. John 4:34.
3. John 12:32.
4. C. A. Dinsmore, *Atonement in Literature and Life*, p. 232; quoted in D. M. Baillie, *God was in Christ* (Faber and Faber, 1948), p. 194.
5. T. S. Eliot, *The Dry Salvages* V, lines 17–21, 29–32, in *The Four Quartets* (Faber and Faber, 1944).
6. Christopher Nolan, *Under the Eye of the Clock* (Weidenfeld and Nicolson, 1987), p. 31.
7. Matthew 5:39.
8. John 18:22f.
9. See C. F. D. Moule, *The Phenomenon of the New Testament* (SCM, 1967), Chapter II.
10. Matthew 25:40.
11. This is the case in all three versions: Acts 9:4; 22:7; and 26:14.
12. Hanan Ashrawi, *This Side of Peace* (Simon and Schuster, 1995), p. 298.
13. Austin Farrer, *A Celebration of Faith* (Hodder and Stoughton, 1970), p. 66.
14. John V. Taylor, *Kingdom Come* (SCM, 1989), p. 86.
15. 2 Corinthians 5:18, 19.

16. Dag Hammarskjöld, *Markings* (ET Faber and Faber, 1964), p. 163.
17. Emmi Bonhoeffer, *The Auschwitz Trials* (St Andrew Press, 1969), p. 47.
18. H. A. Williams, *Jesus and the Resurrection* (Longmans, Green and Co., 1951), p. 65ff.
19. Austin Farrer, *A Celebration of Faith*, p. 89f.
20. George Eliot, *Silas Marner* (1861), chapter 14.
21. Ephesians 1:10.
22. Colossians 1:17.

4

Encouragement

WE merit criticism; we are tickled by flattery; but what we need is encouragement. True encouragement is reassurance grounded in an accurate assessment of who and what we are. It is not flannel, which is just the bland comment of the superficial emerging in such remarks as 'how marvellous you are, and we all admire you'. Nor is it devastating criticism which so latches on to our failures that our capabilities are obscured from us, leaving us shattered and with no strength left to get up and get going again. To be given realistic and well-founded criticism in the context of an overall assurance that we have skills, abilities and grace, can be one of the most invigorating human experiences. Putting this the other way round, we can say that if we are to do anything to help other people to grow and mature then it is encouragement, in the sense of critical appreciation, that we should offer.

True encouragement, which includes critical appreciation grounded in a fair evaluation, is the work of the Spirit of God. Encouragement is not a total or comprehensive description of that work, but it is at least a starting point. St John in his gospel four times uses an unusual word 'Paraclete'[1] for the Spirit of God, and I want here to make the bold suggestion that a defensible working translation of the word is 'the Encourager'. It seems that in classical Greek the word lying behind Paraclete was often used for exhorting soldiers about to go into battle. There is ground for thinking that a Paraclete is someone who puts steel into the faint-hearted, and who makes an ordinary soldier capable of acts of gallantry.[2] The official translators of the Bible are not wholly convinced by this because a glance at the English translations demonstrates that the scholars use different words in an effort to convey the meaning. 'Advocate', 'Counsellor', and 'Comforter' are used by different translators, while some shy away from any attempt to find an English word and stick to a transliteration of the Greek word and just use 'Paraclete'.

It is clear that no one English word can capture the complexity of the word as it is used by St John in his gospel. He sees the Holy Spirit as the personal presence of Jesus in the Christian while Jesus is with the Father, and he links this with the Spirit of God being the Spirit of truth.[3] The concept seems to be that the Spirit of God is present in the individual Christian, assisting us to stand in the presence of God as we are in truth, neither obscuring our weaknesses nor underestimating our potential. Where the scholars vary in their efforts to find the most appropriate word, it is foolish for us to rush in, but can we not say at least that it is not wholly inaccurate to think of the Spirit as the Encourager – the divine presence in us helping us to see ourselves as we truly are, and so enabling us to be who God intends us to be, and presenting us to God as such.

Too many Christians are prevented from attaining their full and free potential because they easily allow their failures to hide from themselves what they are and what, by divine grace, they can become. The saintly Bishop Edward King of Lincoln, writing about the saints, and in doing so unconsciously writing about himself, said:

> Surprise is the true motto of the saints. Good people do not know what they are doing. Good people, as a rule, differ from us ordinary people. Most of us ordinary people know how to be a great deal better than we are, but really good people are generally a great deal better than they know how to be; they are not conscious of being what they are. They are simply what they are, good people, and so they are surprised when the result of their lives at all comes out into view.[4]

Here we have a man, now widely acknowledged to be a saint, showing us how the Spirit of God takes us by surprise, by being with us and in us, enabling and encouraging us to be better than we know how to be. Allowing the Spirit of God to enter into our lives and letting him then draw us into the life of God means that we find a power and strength that we did not know were there. It is ungrateful and ungracious to fail to realise what we can become through the grace of God. Although we must always beware of the arrogance which relies on human achievement, we should be ready to be surprised by God.

There is a powerful moment in John McCarthy's account of his imprisonment in Beirut, when he finds himself transformed by what he decides to call the Good Spirit. McCarthy makes it

clear that he is not, or does not perceive himself to be, a practising or coherent Christian. He was reared in a conventional
and rather formal Christian context, and he disdains any direct
religious experience. Yet he writes tellingly of an experience
which, if it is not religious, is profounder than many experiences
claiming to be so:

> So many of my reflections had left me feeling inadequate that I
> really began to doubt that I could cope alone. One morning
> those fears became unbearable. I stood in the cell sinking into
> despair. I felt that I was literally sinking, being sucked down
> into a whirlpool. I was on my knees, gasping for air, drowning in
> hopelessness and helplessness. I thought that I was passing out.
> I could only think of one thing to say – 'Help me please, oh God,
> help me'. The next instant I was standing up, surrounded by a
> warm bright light. I was dancing, full of joy. In the space of
> a minute, despair had vanished, replaced by boundless opti-
> mism. What had happened? I had never had any great faith,
> despite a Church of England upbringing. But I felt that I had to
> give thanks. But to what? Unsure of the nature of the experience,
> I felt most comfortable acknowledging the Good Spirit which
> seemed to have rescued me. It gave me great strength to carry on
> and, more importantly, a huge renewal of hope – I was going to
> survive. Throughout my captivity I would take comfort from this
> experience, drawing on it whenever optimism and determi-
> nation flagged.[5]

It is dangerous, and perhaps arrogant, to comment on this
significant experience of a man who has faced suffering and
anguish to a degree few others have known, yet can we suggest
that this is a powerful description of an experience of the Holy
Spirit the Encourager? Or may we at least boldly say that here in
our contemporary world is an experience closely parallel to that
which many of us have known in less dramatic circumstances
and in more modest degree: a discovery that the Spirit of God
enters us and our world and gives courage and confidence of
which we did not dream we were capable? We might say that
here is an experience which makes us 'catch our breath'. The
phrase is instructive: is it not a reflection of the experience of
being in-spired? Jesus was born only once, but that birth is re-
enacted and fulfilled in such moments of in-spiration, as the
Spirit of Jesus is breathed again into us and becomes part of our
life today. God, whether we call him the Good Spirit, or the Holy
Spirit, enters our lives and raises us to a new standard of living.
    Another way of expressing this experience is to think in terms

of being 'possessed' by the Spirit of God. This word, and the concept, have been taken over by a certain brand of Christian and can convey that we lose control of ourselves and fall about, shake, or give way to subconscious laughter. These are not typical experiences and can prevent people from acknowledging that many others have a sense of being 'possessed' by God. I can be charged with a responsibility (appointment to a new post, being asked to undertake a specific assignment) which makes me tremble, as I am not sure that I can responsibly undertake a task so patently beyond my ability. In these circumstances I can catch my breath, trust that God will provide the strength that is needed, and then give myself to the work. I may then find that a new calmness or peace comes over me as I recognise that what I am doing is not relying on my fragile human skills but depending on God to raise those skills to a new level of performance.

This sense of being possessed does not mean that I am deeply conscious of God all the time that I am doing what has been asked of me. Rather the reverse: I find myself 'lost', as we say, in the work before me and give myself totally to what is immediately to hand. It is only afterwards that I am able to see what has been happening. A surgeon carrying out a delicate brain operation, an artist working at a painting, a preacher engaged in delivering a sermon, a joiner concentrating on the grain of his wood – in such instances the human mind has to be given wholly to the work before it. Yet the creative work, as we reflect afterwards, was inspired.

This experience of the Spirit in us may be considered further under certain headings suggested by the New Testament – freedom, love, vision and transparency.

I

Most of us long to be free, not just free to do what we like, but to be freed from those parts of ourselves, sometimes so deep within us as to be beyond easy reach, which hold us back. Some feel trapped by their past, others by their shortcomings or their addictions. Many are held back because they have cast themselves in the wrong role: for some reason they have decided what kind of person they want or ought to be, and are hampered and frustrated because they find themselves to be someone different. Others are held back because they know that they have not become the person that they know God wants them to

be: the short word for this is 'sin', falling short of the glory of
God.

There is nothing new in this sense of being held back and
longing to be set free; it is common to most of us to feel
imprisoned by some aspect of ourselves. Centuries ago the
psalmist expressed it for us: 'Bring my soul out of prison, that I
may give thanks unto thy name: which thing if thou wilt grant
me, then shall the righteous resort unto my company.'[6] The
psalmist shrewdly moves from the deep desire for freedom to
acknowledge that the truly liberated person attracts others.

It is the Spirit of God who sets us free. In writing to the
congregation at Corinth, St Paul refers to freedom in connection
with the Spirit of God: 'Where the Spirit of the Lord is, there is
freedom.'[7] The phrase arises in a context where there is a rigorous argument about the difference between God's new
covenant with humanity and the old covenant. The freedom
Paul has in mind at this point seems to be freedom from sin, the
written law and death. Without engaging in detail with that
argument, it is fair to say that St Paul argues here (and
elsewhere) that through the birth, life and death of Jesus, God
has entered this world and engaged directly with our concerns,
aspirations and problems. If in response to that action of God
we allow the Spirit that inspired Christ to inspire us, then we
are set free – not to do as we like, but to live the life of Christ.

We are not offered a licence to go our own way, but freedom
to be unashamedly ourselves and to become the person God
wants us to be. It is this freedom which liberates us to move
with moral and spiritual suppleness as we enter into Christ.
Some Christians show signs of being so anxious about their
moral weakness and failure that they look like spiritual marion-
ettes, with moral splints applied to their limbs so that they
move with a stiffness and distorted awkwardness that attracts
attention to themselves as they self-consciously push one limb
in front of the other. True Christians are not stiff and self-
conscious, but people who forget themselves and are liberated
by the awareness that God has made them who they are, and
they can relax and be themselves – foibles, frailties and all – but
transformed by Christ and his Spirit. All our abilities are gifts,
as we still say in common speech. That not only secures a truth,
but it also provides a clue to integrated living. When we see our
skills and abilities as gifts, we do not take credit to ourselves, or
become arrogant and contemptuous of others. In the course of
cutting the congregation at Corinth down to size, St Paul wrote,
'Who sees anything different in you? What have you that you

did not receive? If then you received it, why do you boast as if it were not a gift?'[8] It is by recognising our dependence on God's generosity and continuing support, that we are released to be accurate about our skills and weaknesses, grateful to God and trusting in his continuing inspiration. That is what sets us free.

The old prophet Jeremiah had seen this obvious distinction between the freedom that comes from the Spirit of God within and the stiffness that comes from slavishly following a written code of behaviour. He hears God speaking:

> I will put my law within them, and I will write it upon their hearts: and I will be their God and they shall be my people. And no longer shall each man teach his neighbour and each his brother, saying 'Know the Lord', for they shall all know me, from the least of them to the greatest, says the Lord.[9]

We are not set free by the presence of the Spirit from all moral codes and commandments. They are still needed, but their context and significance are now transformed. Commandments are not a set of commands which we have to obey if we are to make any spiritual or moral progress, but an assurance of the style and standard of life that we can enjoy when we allow the Spirit to enter our hearts. We can enter the freedom of Christ. He was still constrained by outward circumstance – by soldiers, nails, pain and anguish, and indeed by his relationship with God – but he was spectacularly free to reach out as the Man of Freedom. John Barton comments perceptively about freedom:

> The truly free man, it was said, was not the person who had the wealth and leisure to organise his own life, but the person whose inner resources enabled him to cope with whatever chances and hardships life threw in his path . . . Jesus was more than a Stoic philosopher. In him we do not see the integrity and self-composure of the person with an iron will and a proper sense of his own dignity, who can afford to despise even his torturers . . . But Jesus' greatness is not precisely of that kind. Jesus' freedom is expressed not in detachment and austere contempt for his murderers, but in love and compassion for them, even for them, especially for them.[10]

It is this liberality of love and compassion that makes Christ such an attractive as well as a demanding person. That liberality of love should be the mark of the Christian and of the church at large.

One of the gains in the recent life of the church has been the sense of freedom which the charismatic movement has given to traditions other than its own. Worship among charismatics is less structured and freer than in the more traditional congregations, but even those who are more staid in their acts of worship have as a result of the charismatic movement begun to be less constrained. We do not need to concentrate overmuch on those liberations in the context of worship that seem to be so valued by the charismatics, because the surer gain is a wider and deeper sense of freedom which is now permeating the church as a whole.

II

We can consider the work of the Spirit also in terms of love. In the western church we have laid stress on academic rigour, doctrinal definition, and an intelligent apologetic for the Christian faith. All of these are undoubtedly important, but they are not the only way towards comprehending eternal truth and experiencing God. The fourteenth-century author of the *Cloud of Unknowing* reminds us that we can know God through love more reliably than through the intellect:

> All rational beings, angels and men, possess two faculties, the power of knowing and the power of loving. To the first, to the intellect, God who made them is for ever unknowable, but to the second, to love, he is completely knowable, and that by every separate individual.[11]

It is, then, through love that we can best comprehend God, and this is because love is one of the principal gifts of the Spirit.

St Paul wrote that the love of God has been poured into our hearts through the Holy Spirit who has been given to us.[12] Love is a slippery word much and widely used. Here we are using the word in a defined sense. In thinking of the love of God we mean that love which we see generously given in the creation of the world, extravagantly given by Christ in his life and death, and repeatedly given to us by the Spirit as he enters us and our world.

In the gospels[13] a man asks Jesus 'Which commandment is the first of all?' Jesus replies, 'You shall love the Lord your God' and 'You shall love your neighbour as yourself'. In those words, it is sometimes said, we have the quintessence of Christian life. But that is hardly true. For one thing, the first command, 'Thou shalt love the Lord thy God' was known by every Jew. He was required to recite it (and other passages from Scripture) every morning and evening. When the Jew performed this ritual in his daily prayer, the rabbis said he took upon himself the yoke of the kingdom. So when a Jew said day after day, 'Thou shalt love the Lord thy God' he thought of himself as being harnessed to God's plough, putting himself at God's disposal, being taken wherever God wanted.

This is taken further by Jesus where he is recorded as saying, 'A new commandment I give to you, that you love one another; even as I have loved you, that you also love one another.'[14] The setting in St John's gospel is the night before the crucifixion. There is not much doubt about what Christ means: 'Having loved his own who were in the world, he loved them to the end.'[15] Love of that order of total self-giving is the love of Christ. Here is the 'yoke' of the kingdom, that discipline which sets us free to enter that self-giving love and to let it pass through us to others. And St Paul wrote, 'The love of Christ controls us':[16] once we are seized by the fact that Christ died for all, we simply have to spread the word. The love of God has been poured into our hearts through his Spirit who has been given to us.

When we consider love it is worth noting that loving is not the same as liking. We do not have to like all the people we care for. I do not like parsnips or custard skin; in fact they may make me feel sick. And some people have much the same effect on me as do parsnips and custard skin. I do not and cannot *like* them. To force ourselves into liking someone we do not like is to try to induce an emotion which has no roots. It may flourish for a while but it will soon wither away. To love a person we do not have to like them. We do have to value and treasure them as valued individuals in the sight and love of God. We have to be aware of their needs and hopes and potential and not be blown off course by our own feelings.

Nor must we confuse love with benevolence. Benevolence is a detached and general well-wishing. Love is a burning zeal that requires each person to be infinitely prized. A headmaster can be sincerely benevolent and not love any of his pupils. That is all right for a headmaster. But a father who is benevolent to his whole family but who loves none of his children does not again our respect.

Our minds have subconsciously accepted divine benevolence in place of divine love because we are influenced unawares by the kind of society in which we live. We have been reared in the welfare state and we tend to think of a welfare God, a God of detached benevolence, a divine ombudsman to whom we can turn for redress when all else has failed. If we believe in a God of benevolence we shall ourselves become benevolent – taking the line of least resistance, tolerating substandard behaviour, and talking in terms of generalised ideals. Love, on the other hand, is vigorous though gentle, compassionate yet with a cutting edge.[17]

Fire makes some things red hot without harming them, but consumes other things to dust and ashes; so love in the Spirit is a zealous burning which shares itself with the good and consumes the bad away. This is another way of saying that part of divine love is wrath. God's love for us is so strong that his wrath can be felt as well. We live in a generation which has tended to explain away the wrath of God and the anger of Christ. Wrath and anger do not fit into a tolerant Christian scheme, nor go with a God of divine benevolence, but they are inevitable in a God of burning love. The depth and quality of that love of God are to be reflected in our attitudes. Our job is to hold firmly and tenaciously to the heart of the gospel, to adhere to clear moral standards, to be unashamed in following the disciplines of discipleship, and to take on ourselves the yoke of the kingdom, but at the same time to be extravagant in our devotion to God and infinitely compassionate in our engagement with individuals.

This love of God which is poured into our hearts through the Holy Spirit who has been given to us enables us to give generously in spirit beyond the normal human capacity. Brother Ramon, an Anglican Franciscan friar, has described the way in which he became aware of divine love being far more extensive than human love. This was in a period when he was living as a hermit in the woods and the barrenness of winter opened his eyes to the warmth of the love of God:

> Yesterday I went walking into the Batcombe woods; the trees were stark and bare, the brown leafy mould was soft beneath my feet, and I felt the sadness and glory of human love, and how it reflects and reaches for that which it symbolises in the source and fullness of the divine Love. So much of my understanding of love is reflected in the cosmos, and the February solitude captured the way in which my own pilgrimage manifests the sad absence of my Lord. And yet, though the sun filtered weakly through the trees, and the soft wind was cold, the whole atmosphere held promise, and I could feel the soft breathing of the life beneath my feet. All this is within my own heart – and in the solitude I *feel* the response which I merely *believe* when surrounded by the busyness down below in the friary.[18]

Just as Jesus saw divine truth through village events and stories, Brother Ramon sees the strength and vigour of the love of

God beneath the February deadness and brittleness of so much human love. Pondering the experience of human love can enable us to see deeper into the love of God. The person who has penetrated deeply here is the poet John Donne:

> Love is as strong as death, but nothing is as strong as either, and both love and death met in Christ. How strong and powerful then should instruction be, that comes to you from both of these, the love and death of Jesus.[19]

The Spirit that is given to us is not just an unattached Good Spirit, but specifically the Spirit of Christ, and it is his love shown in and through his death that should, by the work of his Spirit, increasingly pervade our attitude to others and to the world. John Donne wrote elsewhere:

> Whom God loves, he loves to the end: and not to their end, and to their death; but to his end, and his end is that he might love them more.[20]

These are sentences of such profundity that they are as well used for prayer and approaching God in love as for intellectual understanding.

The love that is in Christ is comprehensive, drawing into itself the manifestations of love that have been observed in so many of the great Christians. Fr Raymond Raynes once said:

> In Jesus I see the gentle compassionate love of Mary, the passionate love of St Paul, the impulsive love of St Peter, the sweet reasonable love of St John, the agonizing love of St Francis, the persevering love of St Theresa, the fierce love of the soldier saints – Ignatius – the reflective love of an Aquinas, the innocent love of the child saints – they are diverse expressions of Love, with this one thing in common, their hearts were at one with the heart of Jesus . . . pouring out themselves in Love – because it is the essence of love to share and to give.[21]

For many it is the pragmatic expression of that love in the unlovely parts of the world towards people who seem to have been left uncared for that is the most compelling and convincing evidence of the strength of the love of God. Mother Theresa, who, despite a certain frailty of appearance, has confounded bureaucracy, moved mountains, and loved where there seemed nothing to love, has been the embodiment of the love of God in the contemporary world. She has written, 'Only draw your love from a deep enough source, and sooner or later those whom you love will soon recognise where it comes from.'[22]

This love which is so releasing comes from the Spirit of Christ who draws us into the love of God. That love given by God draws love out of us in adoration of him. To enter that love requires sustained prayer and devotion, symbolised in a comment from Aelred of Rievaulx:

> Break the alabaster of your heart and whatever devotion you have, whatever love, whatever desire, whatever affection, pour it all out upon your Bridegroom's head, while you adore the man in God and God in the man.[23]

III

Our understanding and experience of the Spirit can also be deepened if we reflect for a moment on the way the Spirit opens our eyes. At the beginning of the gospel accounts Jesus is baptised. The Spirit descends, symbolised as a dove, evoking memories of the dove at the time of God's first covenant with humanity after the flood. Mark's account states that Jesus' eyes were opened, so to speak, to see this action of the Spirit. Luke appears to enlarge this to imply that the people generally were able to see.[24] In their different ways the evangelists imply that the presence of the Spirit opens people's eyes. In his ministry Jesus is approached by blind people who ask for their sight back, and he opens their eyes. At St Paul's conversion something like scales fell from his eyes, and he began to see with a new clarity. It is the work of God's Spirit to open our eyes and to give us a vision of his kingdom.

Today we are often immersed in our own affairs and the details of our daily diary. We watch with care where our next step will be, and do not often lift up our eyes to the hills to see where we are heading. So we become engrossed in a succession of isolated events without a clear end or aim. Those who catch our imaginations are often those who are as engrossed as we are, yet able to hold their heads high and to have vision, sometimes a clear vision of the ultimate goal, and sometimes just the capacity to look at the everyday and to see through it to the eternal. As the Spirit of God opens our eyes, we see colour and texture in the world around us where before things seemed grey and flat. The person touched by the Spirit is alert to seeing grace in people who are handicapped, and beauty in those who are designated ugly. His eyes are opened to new possibilities in the world around as he sees through the temporal to the eternal, through the earthy to the heavenly.

In John McCarthy's dramatic account of his incarceration in Beirut to which we have already referred, there are treasured moments of illumination which catch him unawares. One such moment of vision is in the mundane circumstances of being taken, blindfolded, to the bathroom:

> Another poignant moment came when Ali [his guard] was taking me to the bathroom a few days later. On the way back he stopped me in the guards' room and took me over to one of the beds. I looked beneath my blindfold and saw a baby wriggling about. I knelt down in awe. I put a hand out to touch a little foot – more wriggling and a gurgle . . . Here in this place of fractured, tortured minds and morals, was a living image of innocence, ignorant of the purpose of the place and of what his father did to other men in the name of God. I cherished those few seconds. It was a new beginning in one life and allowed me to believe that I, too, would be able to begin again.[25]

This capacity for seeing eternal meaning in the events before our eyes often goes with the capacity for having a vision of the ultimate goal. Leslie Hunter, at one time Bishop of Sheffield, was an innovative, if sometimes ruthless, pioneer and visionary. At the end of his life he had become ready to move on, and looked further ahead to the city of God; he used to turn back to the words from Browning which had been with him for many years:

> . . . when suddenly its spires afar
> Flashed through the circling clouds; you may conceive
> My transport. Soon the vapours closed again,
> But I had seen the city, and one such glance
> No darkness could obscure.[26]

IV

Having briefly considered the work of the Spirit under the heading of freedom, love and vision, let us finally consider transparency to the Light. To find that coherence in life and in God which makes moral and spiritual sense of our lives we need to allow the Spirit to permeate our lives, and to let the glory of God shine through us. There has to be a transparency in all that we do so that the light and love of God can shine through our mists and shadows. Nicholas Mosley wrote of his first impressions of Raymond Raynes, an austere and in some ways turbulent monk:

> I first met Father Raynes when he was Superior of the Com-

munity of the Resurrection . . . I was agnostic. He was unlike any other person I had met in that his great authority did not come from his own personality, but from a transparency to something beyond him. He was a person whom one had either to listen to or to deny; one could not ignore him.[27]

This transparency is succinctly set out for us by Gerard Manley Hopkins when he is writing about our Lady:

> This one work has to do:
> Let all God's glory through.[28]

The Mother of Jesus became who and what she was through yielding herself into the hands of God and allowing the Spirit to enter so that Christ was formed in her: here is the symbol of obedience and total yielding to the Spirit.

In more recent times Dag Hammarskjöld has seen himself being an instrument in the hand of God, and a lens through which his glory can shine on to the world:

> You are not the oil, you are not the air – merely the point of combustion, the flash point where the light is born. You are merely the lens in the beam. You can only receive, give and possess the light as the lens does. If you seek yourself, 'your rights', you prevent the oil and air from meeting in the flame, you rob the lens of its transparency. Sanctity – either to be the Light, or to be self-effaced in the Light, so that it may be born, self effaced so that it may be focused or spread wider.[29]

There is another moment when his yielding to the Spirit of God becomes a prayer:

> Thou takest the pen – and the lines dance. Thou takest the flute – and the notes shimmer. Thou takest the brush – and the colours sing. So all things have meaning and beauty in that space beyond time where thou art. How then can I hold back anything from Thee?[30]

By allowing the work of God's Spirit to permeate our lives, we discover a new freedom. We enter his love, and share a vision of his kingdom. We are transformed by that Spirit so that the glory of God can shine even through our murky and muddled beings. This is no easy matter, nor can it be taken for granted. But it is possible by the grace of God, and that is the surest encouragement of all.

Notes

1. See John 14:16; 14:26; 15:26; 16:7; see also 1 John 2:1.
2. See William Barclay, *More New Testament Words* (SCM, 1958), p. 134f.
3. See R. E. Brown, *The Gospel According to John* (Geoffrey Chapman, 1971), p. 1,135ff.
4. Quoted J. A. Newton, *Search for a Saint: Edward King* (Epworth, 1977), p. 14.
5. John McCarthy and Jill Morrell, *Some Other Rainbow* (Bantam, 1993; Corgi, 1994), p. 66.
6. Psalm 142:9 (Book of Common Prayer).
7. 2 Corinthians 3:17.
8. 1 Corinthians 4:7.
9. Jeremiah 31:33f.
10. John Barton, *Love Unknown*, p. 34f.
11. *Cloud of Unknowing* (Penguin, 1961) p. 55.
12. Romans 5:5.
13. Mark 12:28ff, Matthew 22:35ff, Luke 10:25ff.
14. John 13:34.
15. John 13:1.
16. See 2 Corinthians 5:14.
17. This whole section is much indebted to the lively analysis by Austin Farrer in *Lord I Believe*, chapter 2.
18. Brother Ramon SSF, *A Hidden Fire* (Marshalls, 1985), p. 47f.
19. Quoted in Olive Wyon, *The Grace of the Passion* (SCM Press, 1959), p. 53. Donne is himself quoting from the Song of Solomon 8:6.
20. This sentence was used at a memorial service in Trinity College, Cambridge, for Bishop John A. T. Robinson, 11 February 1984.
21. Quoted in Nicholas Mosley, *The Life of Raymond Raynes*, p. 100.
22. Quoted in a CMS *Newsletter*, December 1975.
23. St Aelred, *A Rule of Life for a Recluse*, in *Treatises and the Pastoral Prayer* (Cistercian Publications, Michigan, 1971), quoted in Grace Jantzen, *Julian of Norwich* (SPCK, 1987), p. 31.
24. Mark 1:10, Luke 3:21f.
25. John McCarthy, *Some Other Rainbow*, p. 98.
26. *Paracelsus* (1835).
27. Nicholas Mosley, *The Life of Raymond Raynes* (Faith Press, 1961), Preface.
28. Gerard Manley Hopkins, 'The Blessed Virgin compared to the Air we Breathe'.

29. Dag Hammarskjöld, *Markings* (ET Faber and Faber, 1964), p. 133.
30. Dag Hammarskjöld, *Markings*, p. 105.

5

Held Together

HOLIDAYS abroad are marginally spoilt by that sense of duty that requires us to send picture postcards to our forlorn friends still in dull old England. We find a card and then scrawl on the back 'visited this place yesterday and enjoyed the open view across the bay to the majestic mountains beyond'. When we write that we admit quietly to ourselves that the card means more to us than it does to the person to whom the card is delivered. We have seen the view, and so to us the picture is an adequate reminder. If our little Englander has not seen the actuality and has only the picture, the card does not mean much; it simply cannot do the scenery justice, and is just one more card from more fortunate friends in the Mediterranean. There is no doubt that a postcard functions best as an *aide-mémoire*.

Sometimes I attend a talk and am impressed by the speaker: his mastery of the subject, the lucidity of the analysis, the aptness of the quotations, the humour, the wit – marvellous, I think. Then inevitably, in that embarrassed silence when the chairman asks for questions, someone will ask if the text of the speaker's talk could be circulated. Some devoted typist labours away with a typescript altered by scribbles, with tape recorder, and other modern gadgetry, then sorts it out and sends it round. A week or two later it drops on to my breakfast table. But those typed pages are as dry as unbuttered toast. The fire and spirit and liveliness are not there. There is no interplay of minds, only the bare shape of the words. At best, it is an *aide-mémoire*; at worst, another layer in the waste-paper basket.

Statements about God the Trinity are not the reality, and can only be *aides-mémoire*. They try to encapsulate and remind us of a corporate and accumulated experience. If we regard them as statements or doctrines to be read intellectually, they will not excite the mind or fire the imagination: they will be like unbuttered toast. But if we can see those statements as *aides-mémoire*, black and white cards to remind us of colourful, even glorious, experience, then perhaps they will serve their purpose. The Trinity is not so much a dogma about God as an experience of living in him. The Christian life is the adventure of being drawn into the life and love of God and taking our part in that whole and rounded existence in the heavens.

It is the task of the academic theologians to formulate and scrutinise statements about the Trinity with full intellectual rigour, but their findings are not the end of the matter; they are dependent on and have to be related to the experience of the church and of individual Christians as we grow in our knowledge and love of God. The theologian has no better (but no worse) access to God than does the least educated Christian, and sometimes it is the saints, such as Julian of Norwich, who pray their way into the life of God, who speak more eloquently than do the academics. In one of his poems John Donne neatly makes the point:

> O blessed glorious Trinity,
> Bones to philosophy, but milk to faith.[1]

On the other hand, and especially if for a time we sit light to the academic theologian, we must avoid the trap of triviality. In our attempts to be simple it is easy to be superficial. Michael Ramsey used to say, 'There are two kinds of simplicity. There is the simplicity of the superficial and there is the simplicity of the master mind.'[2] He was himself an example of the master mind: he more than most could enter into the heart of complex ideas and then distil the truth of God and set it out for others to see and share. If, rightly, we go for simplicity, we must try to avoid triviality.

As well as triviality of mind there is a triviality of experience. Some, especially the young in faith, judge that they have grasped the gospel and the truth about God and can explain it all to others with ease and conviction and so bring people to Christ. Worthy though that may be, there is the danger that the knowledge from which they speak is not deeply enough rooted in experienced pain and anguish. Dag Hammarskjöld has some elegant warnings about the risk of superficiality because he was so aware, in his deep spirituality, of how trivial even he could be:

> A blown egg floats well, and sails well on every puff of wind –
> light enough for such performances, since it has become nothing

but a shell; . . . anxious to please – speech without form, words without weight. Mere shells.[3]

And another jotting from his White Book on the same subject:

A modest wish: that our doings and dealings may be of a little more significance to life than a man's dinner jacket is to his digestion. Yet not a little of what we describe as our achievement, is, in fact, no more than a garment in which, on festive occasions, we seek to hide our nakedness.[4]

The treason of the cleric is to trivialise the gospel and package God in easily available quantities, with the result that we lose the mystery and wonder. As any worthy minister ascends the pulpit steps he is trembling: how can he in the few minutes now available to him convey the wonder and mystery of God in modern terms? How can his pint-pot mind contain all the water which flows from the fountain of life? As he pauses on those steps he knows the task of expounding the mystery of God and the majesty of the gospel is beyond him, and he can but pray that through his mundane words and simple sentences somehow God will enable the congregation to enter the mystery of God.

That prayer is the more urgent when a preacher has to open people's minds to the wonder of the Trinity. Yet perhaps the preacher should reflect that the congregation almost certainly have experience of the Trinitarian God even if they have not yet been given the words and mental means of articulating their experience in a way that enables them to see that their life and prayer is trinitarian.

The rudest man or woman who cannot reason about the Trinity may *know* the Trinity more perfectly than some acute theologian who has by heart all the writing of St Athanasius or St Augustine, and all the controversies of the first six centuries.[5]

A sermon or statement about the Trinity is not a new doctrine nor a complex formulation, but a map to help us see our experience in perspective, to discover where we are, and to assist us in seeing where to go next. At the risk, then, of triviality, let us rehearse our experience of God and see the way in which it interlocks and hangs together, and so draws us into a new sense of coherence, integrity and wholeness.

I

The use of words such as 'wholeness' at once recalls the Hebrew idea of *Shalom*. This word which means peace is rooted in the concept of completeness. The Greek equivalent, *eirene*, and the Latin *pax* have more the sense of suspension of strife, or interludes between inescapable tension and war. The Hebrew word by contrast is deeply rooted in the soil of God's wholeness and peace, and it can blossom in the chilly atmosphere of the world only if its roots are drawing sustenance from the earth of God. God's *shalom* or peace is always on offer. God is a God of peace and the normal state of those made in his image is peacefulness.

St Paul begins all his letters with a reference to the peace of God. The characteristic formula is 'Grace to you and peace from God our Father and the Lord Jesus Christ'.[6] The letter to the Hebrews includes reference to 'the God of peace who brought again from the dead our Lord Jesus'.[7] These are patent illustrations of the New Testament recognition that peace is an inherent part of God the Creator and Father.

This *shalom* is brought to us by Christ. Jesus is recorded by St John as saying, 'Peace I leave with you; my peace I give to you; not as the world gives do I give to you. Let not your hearts be troubled, neither let them be afraid.'[8] St Paul in his letter to the Ephesians states boldly that Christ is our peace.[9] So the New Testament writers spell out that the *shalom* of God is embodied for us in the person of Christ who gives us that peace which passes all understanding.

Christ's death on the cross is seen by the New Testament writers as an act of reconciliation and peace, and we have to ensure that his reconciliation and peace pervade the world and overcome the turbulence and divisiveness of humanity. The working out of that in practice is specifically passed on to us[10] through the power and presence of the Spirit. We complete what is lacking in the afflictions of Christ,[11] and the consequential peace is one of the fruits of the Spirit.[12]

Just in this brief summary of the idea of *shalom* in the New Testament we see how the writers' understanding of divine peace is threefold. This is not spelt out in a neat trinitarian formula, but the tide of trinitarian thinking is running firmly just below the surface. What we see here in outline in connection with peace, we can now look at from the angle of human experience.

II

We have inherited language about three persons in one God. But at the time that language was first used in that context 'person' did not mean an individual so much as a particularis-ation of an essence or being. We meet people who at different times wear different hats, as we say. I was once asked to become the vicar of a market town of some 10,000 people. As well as meeting churchwardens and other officials of the congregation, because the town had a strong ecumenical tradition, I was asked to meet the Methodist circuit steward. I also wanted to meet the headmaster of the school where our children might be educated. Because in market towns there is often a constructive relation-ship between the church and the civic authorities, I thought it diplomatic to ask to meet the Mayor. I was gently amused to find that the Mayor, the headmaster and the Methodist circuit steward were the same person, and that amusement of mine was nicely reflected. Each conversation took place in a different context: the nature of the relationship varied on each occasion, the knowledge and understanding gained were different, and the experience of personal encounter was transmuted. It was a pleasantly comic, though serious, series of encounters.

When the ancients were talking of three persons in one God, they meant something more like three particularisations of one being, understood and experienced in different ways, but clearly interrelated. That is different from saying in today's terms that we believe in three persons in one God, and we have to be wary of using ancient terminology when meanings have changed, particularly when different languages are involved.

The weakness of seeing God as three particularisations of one essential being, especially if we simplify this to meeting one person wearing three hats, is of course that it gives inadequate expression to the diversity of our experience of God. We experi-ence God in three ways, not just three distinguishable ways, but in three distinct ways. To that in a moment we must try to do justice, but for the moment our simple model at least secures the truth that we experience one God in different yet personal ways.

Let us take this further. Let us cast our mind back to the experience of a good teacher. There were three aspects of that experience that we can remember. First, he or she was able to open our eyes and minds to the wonders and excitement of a world of which we were aware but whose extent and intricacies we had only vaguely identified. A teacher opens up our minds to the marvel and glory of this world, and also of course to the tragedies and disasters it can contain. A good teacher educates us out of our prejudices, our small-mindedness and limited perception to grasp just how little we know. The young and the partly educated are often confident that they know all the answers. The truly educated person is crystal clear about his ignorance, and is likely to have a developed sense of awe and amazement before the complexities and subtleties of this world. Furthermore, a good teacher will, perhaps without realising it, inspire a sense of wonder about this world as being the place that bears the footprints of God. He will be aware that the world, the inherited knowledge from the past, the prospects for the future, are all a gift delivered into our laps – but delivered wrapped, and he will share with us in the excitement of discovering this gift and making it our own. We might sense that a good teacher is conveying, probably without saying, that this is the Lord's doing and it is marvellous in our eyes.

Second, a good teacher relates what she knows to what we know. If she natters on at us at her superior level, what she says will go clean over our heads. R. H. Tawney once said, 'Clever men are impressed by their differences from their fellows; wise men by their resemblance to them.' The best teachers are those who articulate for us the ideas and understandings that we were groping for ourselves. I was once a member of a sixth form of mathematicians when we were unexpectedly without our teacher through illness. The Head Master swept into our class room, and said, 'I shall have to teach you this morning, and I am going to talk with you about poetry.' The temperature dropped to zero as we pragmatic and not so cultured mathematicians judged that poetry was not our line. The Head Master turned to me and said, 'Now what poetry do you know?' Stunned, I could think of none. 'Well,' the Head Master said, 'let's start with hymns – they are poetry, most of them bad poetry, but poetry nonetheless.' And so he began to open our eyes to a new world, or rather to open our eyes to a world we already knew but had never stopped to see. Surely our experience of a great teacher is that he relates what he knows to what we know, articulating for us what we were still fumbling to identify and see.

Third, our experience of a good teacher leaves us encouraged and even inspired. The teacher who impresses us with his knowledge and depresses us with our ignorance, is a failure. He deskills us, as the jargon has it. If on the other hand we are encouraged, we become aware of what we do know and enthused to understand more. A good teacher is wise rather than clever. So often we develop a love for a subject not because we have an innate interest in it, but rather because our teacher has fired our imagination, shared his excitement with us, taken us with him in his joyous understanding and search. We are caught up in his enthusiasm.

These three aspects of our experience are interlocking but distinct. They are experiences of the same person, and each aspect of that experience relates to and enhances the others. Of course this is no adequate analogy or symbol of the Trinity but it is a point from which to start. John V. Taylor has used a model that is better but perhaps a little more complex:

> The mother living for her children, the scientist committed to a particular search, the liberator dedicated to an oppressed people, the artist giving form to an inner vision, the devotee pursuing the vision of God – each of them is simultaneously in three distinct states of self-awareness, though only fully conscious of one of them at a time. There is the self-giver absorbed in willing the welfare of the children, the discovery of the truth, and so on, fulfilled in pure *generosity*. There is the given self, conscious of the imperative 'I must', fulfilled in *obedience* to it. And there is the 'in-othering' self that is so identified with the child, the work of art, the victims, the presence of God, as to know them from the inside and be fulfilled only in *their fulfilment*.[13]

This model differs from that of the teacher in that the second aspect underlined is obedience rather than identification. This in itself is a reminder that we need differing models which complement and check each other, and prevent any one model becoming the controlling symbol. These analogies may help us to see how our different experiences of God are in the end all experiences of the same Being: they are models of the unity of God, but they are, as we have said, inadequate as expressions of the diversity of our experience. The accumulated wisdom of the church is that our distinct experiences of God are all permanent rather than passing ones which we have one after another; and that each of these experiences is equal in value and significance.

III

In the hope of understanding these latter aspects, let us take a different picture. In order to deal with a significant and complex problem we may get in touch with a firm of consultants which has three partners. They work very closely together, and although each has his own specialism they also try to cover for one another so that if a customer telephones, he should find that in conversing with any one partner he is receiving the wisdom, knowledge and experience of all three. At any one time one of the partners might think it appropriate for the customer to speak to another partner because that partner is more directly and deliberately involved in one specialised part of their activities. The three partners each have their own distinct personality, which we detect as we talk with them, but we note also the intimate co-ordination of their work. This integrated co-ordination might be even closer if two of the partners are married. In a successful marriage the partners do not compromise and suppress their individuality in order to achieve harmony but are able, through deep and devoted sharing, to see issues through one another's eyes to a point where both see life, so to speak, through a common prism.[14]

This picture helps us to see that one experience of God is an experience of a personal being which is permanently distinct from another experience at another time or in another context. It tries to do justice to the traditional terminology of engaging with three persons in one God. It also tries to secure that as we experience God as Father, Son or Spirit, all three experiences are of God in his entirety, not of one aspect of God with other aspects being inaccessible. Although the Father is primarily that person in the Godhead who is creative and powerful, the biblical evidence and the accumulated experience of the church is that the Son and the Spirit also were active in creation. Similarly, in encountering Christ we are meeting the person in the Godhead who was embodied in human terms and transformed this world. But both the Father and the Spirit were engaged in that activity. When today we are aware of being possessed by the strength and Spirit of God, it is not an independent spirit or a semi-detached Good Spirit, but the Spirit of the Father and of Christ that is enthusing us.

If with these varied pictures complementing one another in our minds we now return to the picture of a good teacher we can see how Christ contains within himself all three elements, and so draws us into a deeper understanding of God.

Jesus was a born teacher. He taught by telling stories. That was his genius. And his stories were not just illustrations of metaphysical or theological truths he had worked out beforehand. He used everyday scenes as the lens through which to focus people's minds on God. He opened our minds to the totality of existence, to God. He encapsulated within himself, and crystallised, the three qualities of a good teacher. First, he opened people's minds to the marvel and wonder of this world as he took the simplest things and scenes and set them thinking and wondering. Second, by telling stories he engaged people's minds where they were. He did not talk in abstract terms above people's heads. He told them stories so that they could engage with what he said from the basis of their own experience. Third, he encouraged and stimulated and spurred. People were left asking themselves, what does this mean for me? Who is my neighbour? A rich man went away sorrowful. They found this a hard saying. He did not just impart knowledge to the mind, but impacted on the whole person: he encouraged.

We can put all this in more precise terms: Jesus opened people's minds to God who made this world; he engaged with people where they were – in human terms; and he encouraged by giving them an understanding and experience of the Holy Spirit the Encourager. So in our experience of Jesus through the prayerful study of the gospels, we are already being drawn into the trinitarian life of God. Jesus was himself a human expression of the triple qualities of a teacher: he showed us in his life and words and work the wholeness of God.

This opening of our eyes to the trinitarian life of God by looking more closely at the life of Jesus is set out in the gospel narratives themselves, not only in some places where there are virtually explicit references to the Trinity, but in less obvious but more telling symbols. One such moment of insight is, as we have seen, the baptism of Jesus in the river Jordan. Jesus, who is the human embodiment of God, goes down into the water, which is the element from which all life came. He descends right down into it, perhaps being totally submerged in the water, or, more probably, standing knee- or waist-deep. In either case he indicates his identity with the totality of creation in its most basic and primitive form, water. As he arises out of that element, the heavens are torn open and he sees (and perhaps the people around see) the Spirit of God descending like a dove as a voice speaks from heaven: 'This is my beloved Son, with whom I am well pleased.' In the record of this event we see the interlocking activity of God, and recognise that here is held together what we with our fragmented lives often experience in separation.

IV

The Trinity is not a mystery in the sense of being an intellectual puzzle almost incomprehensible to us. It is the reverse of that: it is a statement that in the life and death of Christ we see clearly set out the essential truth about God, and have an insight into and a foretaste of the trinitarian nature of that God. John Barton has written this:

> Jesus is not the face God likes to show the world; Jesus is what God is really like. The work of the Holy Spirit in our lives is not the work of God's propaganda department; it is the work of God himself . . . Sometimes in the church today this doctrine of the Trinity is presented as a way of emphasising how mysterious God is. But whatever truth there may be in saying that God is mysterious, the doctrine of the Trinity is the very last doctrine that expresses it. For what it declares is that God who is beyond all our conceptions and our power to imagine him *has made himself known* in Jesus and continues to reveal himself through the work of the Spirit in the world; and in these ways that he reveals himself, it is genuinely himself that he reveals, not something less than his true self, not what he wants us to believe, nor what we can stand, but the truth.[15]

Most Christians come to their understanding of God through an encounter with Christ. That is no surprise: he is God directly and deliberately engaging with the human condition, the embodiment of God in human terms. But not all people come to an understanding of God in this way. Evelyn Underhill once wrote:

> You see, I come to Christ through God, whereas quite obviously lots of people come to God through Christ. But I can't show them how to do that – all I know about is the reverse route. The final result, when you have the two terms united, is much the same . . . but the process quite different.[16]

This is important to recognise, particularly in a period when we appear to be moving in some places towards a Jesus-centred church, with much Jesus-worship, and the increasing use of such phrases as 'bringing people to Christ'. It has to be said that many people come to Christ through God, and some through the Spirit. A trinitarian understanding will recognise that there are many different approaches to the rich mystery of God.

It is also a wise part of our tradition about the Trinity that all the persons in the Godhead are equal. Those who approach God through the Spirit, and whose primary experience is charismatic or possession by the Spirit, are not superior to those who approach God through insight into creation and discover through that an experience of the creative power of God; nor are they superior to those whose primary faith results from their reading of the gospel narratives about the person of Jesus. When any Christian appears to be stressing or leaning on one personal experience of God, and that perhaps a strongly individual experience, then he or she needs to reckon with the age-long Christian tradition of God being a Trinity.

In earlier chapters we have rehearsed ways in which we can realise our humanity best by recognising that we are at one with this world, part of the creation, earthy creatures who can be unashamed of our physical and animal nature. Yet this earthy creature that I am is nonetheless made in the image of God. We have noted also how in the person of Jesus we see a new way of looking at the world, which he has transformed by the working out in time and history of his natural love and care for all that is. We have noted also how the Spirit that worked in Christ has been poured into our hearts and made us capable of a quality and standard of life of which we did not think we were capable. We are now arguing that these are interlocking experiences of one God whose desire is to draw us into his coherent and integrated life.

The language of personality and personalness is vital. We know and experience God in personal ways, not as a distant and elderly father figure, nor as unleaded gasoline which keeps us running on automatic spiritual drive. We have experience of him in essentially personal terms, known most clearly when we read of the impact of the person of Christ on those who met him face to face, and when we relive those stories and find ourselves caught up in them. So it is vitally important to retain the language of the personality and personalness of God.

Furthermore the ancients spoke not only of the personality of God but of personality *in* God. They were trying to say that God is relational and complete in himself. The ancients meant that God does not *need* others. He may want us, but he does not need us. His love for us is an expression of generosity, not of necessity. There is full life in God. There is full love in God. It is into that life and love that we are drawn and the point of entry seems to differ for each individual. Some see a landscape, sense the riches of nature for all its cruelty and blemishes, and yet find themselves drawn into a sense that this world is a gift from God, and so they enter into that world and through it discover God himself. Others turn to the pages of the gospels and find themselves there in the stories that Jesus told, or engaged in the actions of Christ, and they are drawn towards and into that compelling figure who is the very expression of the mind of

God. Others hear a Mozart symphony, or are caught up in some other work of art, and are taken out of themselves into a spiritual world; or through the experience of tragedy find themselves caught up almost against their will into an experience of re-creation by the Spirit of resurrection at work in our world.

For many it is the practice of prayer which enables us to enter into the life of the Trinity. When we start to pray we are aware of our inadequacy and the distractions which break up our efforts at sustained concentration. It is at this point that we become aware of the Spirit of God entering our disjointed hearts:

> The Spirit helps us in our weakness; for we do not know how to pray as we ought, but the Spirit himself intercedes for us with sighs too deep for words. And he who searches the hearts of men knows what is the mind of the Spirit, because the Spirit inter-cedes for the saints according to the will of God.[17]

We find that we are being prayed in by the Spirit. As we are drawn to recognise the reality of Christ, we know that this is the work of God rather than any attainment of ours: 'No one can say "Jesus is Lord" except by the Holy Spirit.'[18] We are aware that Christ shares our humanity with us, and as he knows how to pray, so it is his prayers into which we are drawn and which carry us before the majesty of God. Because like Christ we are human, we pray not as disembodied spirits, but as earthy creatures bringing with us all the jumbled baggage of this world, speaking on behalf of the created universe.

This prayer will sometimes, perhaps often, be an unrewarding experience, where the clouds are grey and the way is dark. That is no surprise. Prayer is not and never will be all excitement and consciousness of delight: Christ trod the stony road to Calvary with only occasional comfort at unexpected moments from people standing by. If we enter into Christ we move into a life that is demanding and exacting, although also rich in hope and promise. Steadily we are brought into the presence of the majesty and glory of God and find ourselves taken up into the life of the Trinity. Most of the considered prayers of the church take us through this route, not least the great prayer of thanksgiving in the eucharist. The mere fact that we become aware of entering into the life and love of God forces us to acknowledge and try to lay aside those burdens of sin and failure which are no worthy parts of such a divine existence.

To give all this more elegant expression, it is again to the poets we must turn:

Lord, who hast formed me out of mud,
    And hast redeemed me through thy blood,
    And sanctified me to do good;

Purge all my sins done heretofore;
    For I confess my heavy score,
    And I will strive to sin no more.

Enrich my heart, mouth, hands in me,
    With faith, with hope, with charity;
    That I may run, rise, rest with thee.[19]

The first stanza here firmly roots the poetic prayer in the Trinity who makes, redeems and sanctifies. A consequence of having a clearer idea of God as a Trinity of persons is that it enables us to see more constructively the world in which we live and the relationships of human persons within it. If we have a vision of God as a coherent being complete in himself yet with distinctive aspects, then we can more confidently acknowledge that God loves not because he needs to or because he yearns for affection and appreciation as we do: he creates, loves and empowers of his own generosity. Our gratitude to him is the greater as a result of seeing this generosity as an essential part of his being.

Second, we see how he holds distinctive elements within his own being in such a way that his life is enriched by his being a diversity in unity. Many of the pressures in our society, as well as innate tendencies within our human make-up, push us towards being defensive about others different from ourselves or fearful of being forced to conform to a standard pattern. We are sometimes, for instance, mistakenly made to think that everyone in the church should agree on everything and 'present a common front'. At other times we resent being 'containerised' and pressed into a corporate box with no freedom to express hesitations or modifications about what the church as a whole is saying. Yet in the Trinity we see God living with and through a diversity from which all too often we shy away.

Third, we can look with fresh eyes at our own fragmentariness. We are aware, as we have seen, of being several people ourselves: we are 'some twenty several men each several hour'.[20] But God, it seems, can hold persons in a perfect and enriching unity. By entering more fully and firmly into the life of God, we are drawn into a glorious unity which transcends our fragmented humanity.

There are many ways in which to start to enter the life of God. Once there we discover a new world of experience. As we reflect on that experience of God we find that we are more aware of the Trinity and more part of it than we might ever have expected had we perceived the Trinity largely as an intellectual puzzle.

Notes

1. John Donne, 'The Litanie', stanza IV.
2. This remark was often made in conversation. There is reference to the idea in Michael Ramsey's *Durham Essays and Addresses* (SPCK, 1956), p. 28.
3. Dag Hammarskjöld, *Markings* (ET Faber and Faber, 1964), p. 52.
4. Ibid., p. 53.
5. Thomas Hancock, *Christ and the People: Sermons on the Obligations of the Church to the State and to Humanity* (1875), p. 304.
6. Romans 1:7.
7. Hebrews 13:20.
8. John 14:27.
9. Ephesians 2:14.
10. 2 Corinthians 5:18.
11. Colossians 1:24.
12. Galatians 5:22.
13. John V. Taylor, *The Christlike God* (SCM Press, 1992), p. 123.
14. This analogy is suggested by David Brown, *The Divine Trinity*, (Duckworth, 1985), p. 300.
15. John Barton, *Love Unknown* (SPCK, 1990), p. 74.
16. Charles Williams (ed), *The Letters of Evelyn Underhill* (Longmans, Green and Co., 1943), p. 206.
17. Romans 8:26ff. See also *We Believe in God* (A report of the Doctrine Commission of the Church of England) (Church House Publishing, 1987), chapter 7.
18. 1 Corinthians 12:3.
19. George Herbert, 'Trinitie Sunday'.
20. See the quotation from George Herbert in chapter 1.

6

Entering God in Prayer

PRAYER is allowing ourselves to be drawn into God – periods when we open ourselves to God in the hope 'that we may evermore dwell in him and he in us' as the Prayer of Humble Access from the Anglican Communion Service puts it so succinctly.

Many people say that they do not pray, or that they do not know how to pray, or that priests and ministers rarely teach them how to pray. Others pray out of long habit but are shy of admitting it, and are not at all confident that they are praying as they should, fearing that their prayer has not grown since they first embarked on the practice many years ago. In the much maligned 1960s Alan Ecclestone wrote a brief pamphlet[1] on prayer, the significance of which is remarked on in the biography of him by Tim Gorringe. Ecclestone urges people not to delay praying until they have worked out a theory of prayer and identified what it is they are doing and why, but rather to recognise that they are probably already praying. It is wiser to pray and discover, than to hesitate and puzzle, because 'prayer is not a problem to be solved but a venture to be lived'.[2] Ecclestone gave at least one generation of people encouragement by helping them to recognise that by identifying commonly experienced moments and dwelling on them, we are already beginning to pray. If we take some daily experiences and hold them long enough to savour them, we can find ourselves moving simply into prayer.

There are, for instance, moments of gladness when we feel that life is so infinitely worth living that we just want to say thank you. Sometimes it is a day of exquisite spring sunshine and a sparkling landscape; sometimes a human relationship which warms and encourages; sometimes it is an intellectual stimulus or an artistic experience: any of these may thrill and make us bubble with gratitude that life is so rich and infinitely worthwhile. A child will often feel gratitude for something but may all too easily say nothing and so appear to take what he has been given for granted. He then has to be helped, and often disciplined, to say 'thank you', to ensure that his gratefulness is recognised by him and by others. We seem to need a comparable discipline which savours these moments of gladness and gratitude and turns them into a deliberate expression of gratitude to God.

> What is here prompted by a spontaneous recognition of the good thing encountered now needs to be used as the willed basis for praying when we come to sit down or kneel down to reflect on a day's experience.[3]

By using occasional moments of joy or excitement and holding on to them, we can turn them into prayer. The psalmist, as so often, has been here before us: 'This is the Lord's doing: and it is marvellous in our eyes. This is the day which the Lord hath made: we will rejoice and be glad in it.'[4]

There are moments when we feel the need for help, because we are frightened, anxious, distressed, in pain or perplexed. We can turn these occasions of feeling 'oh, help' into held moments of prayer. Some may have experienced lying in a hospital bed in severe pain which seems to suck the whole being into its vortex. Sleep becomes impossible and the only available human reaction seems to be 'Oh God!'. Others will know the devastation of a sudden illness or death in the family, or the break up of a marriage. In such circumstances we can feel cornered or near to panic, and if we dared we would just scream for help. There is no shame in turning these moments of devastation into cries to God for help. 'Save me, O God,' wrote the psalmist, 'for the waters are come in even unto my soul. I stick fast in the deep mire, where no ground is: I am come into deep waters, so that the floods run over me.'[5]

Ecclestone might well have added here that close to these moments there are times when we recognise that we have made a mess of a situation – by losing our cool, by talking overmuch rather than listening, or by striving to impose our will rather than engaging with a different view – and we instinctively feel, 'what a mess' or 'what a pig's ear I have made of that'. These are moments when we can acknowledge failure and reflect on the refreshing power of forgiveness: 'Have mercy upon me, O God, after thy great goodness: according to the multitude of thy mercies do away mine offences. Wash me throughly from my wickedness: and cleanse me from my sin. For I acknowledge my faults: and my sin is ever before me.'[6]

There are also moments of exhaustion – sheer physical tiredness, or a sense that we have done all we can and we just have to leave it at that. These are moments when we can let go – 'Into thy hands O Lord I commit my spirit'.[7] Again the psalmist thought in these terms: 'Commit thy way unto the Lord, and put thy trust in him . . . Hold thee still in the Lord, and abide patiently upon him.'[8]

> What we are doing in this kind of praying is of quite immense importance and is the necessary counterpart to all our striving, all our pleas for help, all our enjoyment, all our conscious addressing of ourselves to the demands of living. 'The night cometh' and it matters a great deal whether its inevitable coming fills us with a sense of panic and emptiness, or becomes an occasion for utter relief in letting go ourselves trustfully like a child dropping off to sleep.[9]

Those who have allowed prayer to become arid or dead, or who have never yet started seriously on this pilgrimage, can follow Ecclestone's simple but shrewd guidance and begin on this 'venture to be lived'. Others will have been praying for many years but may not yet have perceived prayer as entering into the life and love of God, and it is to that particular understanding of prayer that we now turn.

I

Some writers on prayer advise that we should empty our minds of all earthly encumbrance, leave our domestic and employment anxieties behind and enter into the peace of God. This is unrealistic. Current anxieties and aspirations have become part of what we are at that moment, and if we are to pray we shall pray in and through the concerns and hopes which dominate our minds and hearts. The masters of the spiritual life in their writings often use the term 'recollection'. It does not in this context mean memory, but to be re-collected, that is, to be brought back into an integrated unity. Our anxieties and aspirations can pull us apart, but if they are re-collected now round a focal point, they can be held together. So instead of allowing all our sharp concerns to continue to fragment us, the practice of recollection is drawing all these concerns together, valuing each against the gold standard of true humanity, which is Christ, and finding a new unity within ourselves and in God.

We are all aware of the disintegrating effect of distractions as we try to pray, but we should not be surprised nor overwhelmed by them. To be human is to be distracted and fragmented, and we cannot in one sense be otherwise. So we come before God as disintegrated creatures asking that his wholeness may permeate our beings. Gerard Hughes writes:

> The opening verse of the Bible, 'Now the earth was a formless void, there was darkness over the deep, and God's Spirit hovered over the water', is describing a present state of affairs, not a past event, and when I pray from the Scriptures, I am letting the Spirit of God hover over the chaos and darkness of my being.[10]

This practice of recollection is a sustained discipline to be distinguished from free-wheeling or idling before God. George Eliot gives us a teasing picture of the way in which we can empty our minds and leave them empty. One of her characters

> spent the evening in the solitude of the smaller drawing room, where, with various new publications on the table, of the kind a gentleman may like to have at hand without touching, he employed himself (as a philosopher might have done) in sitting meditatively on a sofa and abstaining from literature – political, comic, cynical, or romantic. In this way hours may pass surprisingly soon, without the arduous invisible chase of philosophy; not from love of thought, but from hatred of effort.[11]

Recollection is not being vacant before God but requires persistent effort – to pull ourselves together, and to hold steady in the healing love of God. Dag Hammarskjöld has a terse reminder: 'Your cravings as a human animal do not become a prayer just because it is God whom you ask to attend to them.'[12] Recollection, then, is an art which like all other art presupposes a discipline. It is not the business of discarding those concerns which at this moment make us what we are, but the art of holding steady before God, bringing all our diverse concerns into a common sense of direction. If this proves more demanding and at times less rewarding than we had hoped, then we hold hard, knowing that however thin and tenuous our prayer may feel, God is there waiting to draw us in. Many who are masters of prayer have their arid and depressing periods. Even if we wander off, God remains; if we feel arid and dry, the fountain of life is still there. In this context R. S. Thomas's poem 'Folk Tale' is re-assuring:

> Prayers like gravel
>   flung at the sky's
> window, hoping to attract
>   the loved one's
> attention. But without
>   visible plaits to let
> down for the believer
>   to climb up,
> to what purpose open
>   that far casement?
>   I would
> have refrained long since
>   but that peering once
> through my locked fingers
> I thought that I detected
>   the movement of a curtain.[13]

A more explicitly biblical word of encouragement comes from Lancelot Andrewes, who wrote, drawing on other writers, these words:

> If he (Jesus) prayed who was without sin, how much more becometh it a sinner to pray? God hears the heart not the voice: we do more by groans than words. Christ groaned for this reason, to set us an example of groaning.[14]

This comment from a great spiritual master moves us to recognise that we do not necessarily use words in prayer. It is often helpful and appropriate to use words and we can derive enormous assurance and strength from the well-tried prayers of the past, including prayers written by the spiritual giants such as Lancelot Andrewes himself, yet words are not themselves the prayer. Robert Llewellyn has a simple picture of the place of words:

> Real prayer lies beyond the words in the inclination and the offering of the heart, and the function of the words is to set the heart free to pray. The words may be seen as the banks of a river enabling it to remain deep and flowing. Without the banks the waters would scatter and become shallow and even stagnant. A similar danger is open to prayer when the framework in which it freely flows is removed. Yet the prayer is not the framework but lies beyond. And just as when the river flows into the sea the banks are left behind, so when prayer flows more deeply into God, the words, having served their purpose, will drop away.[15]

Silence therefore is an integral part of prayer, for the words having done their job can drop away. Many public acts of worship fail to recognise this and are too relentlessly wordy; those leading public worship should allow space and silence for the spirit of prayer to move, without always trying to fence it in with verbiage. Congregations sometimes find the torrent of words in our liturgies to be exhausting. If we do use words they may in this context have to do more work than is expected of them in normal conversation or writing. Donald Allchin has written:

> God can only speak to us, and we can only speak to God, and of God, in words which our human life has given to us. Because those words are always too small, too limited, too fragile to express the fullness of his being and his joy, we have to seek ways by which we may expand them, allow them to carry more weight, to hold together a greater wealth of meaning and experience than they would normally do. This is one reason why much of the language of faith and prayer is the language of poetry, language which is, as we say, inspired.[16]

That is well said, and reminds us why so many people still want to use the well-tried resonant prayers of the past which have stronger tones and rhythms than some more recently composed prayers seem able to attain. Those stronger and evocative words are often the gateway to a productive silence in the presence of God.

II

Silence is a natural and integral part of prayer. It is not negative, a mere absence of words, but a positive and created space in which we can hear more clearly what the world is saying, what is going on in our minds and hearts, and what God may be saying to us in our predicament. If we stay still and try listening to silence we discover that silence is not silent at all, but contains its own rhythms and patterns. We can hear the ticking of the clock, the distant hum of the traffic, the song of a bird. We find ourselves entering more fully into the depth of the given moment. So in prayer we discover a richness and deeper awareness of the sound and rhythm of life and of God. Austin Farrer makes the point with his usual powerful imagery:

> Prayer is something like that – listening to silence; and directly you try, you find that silence is not silent at all. In the silence of

the mind there are so many drums beating: noisy rhythms of self-conceit, of resentment, of lust, not to mention the busy intellect tapping out themes which amuse or which worry it; each of these rhythms competing for your attention, and setting you on to dance its peculiar tune. But you must push them aside and go deeper into silence, until you can hear that rhythm which, although it may not be the loudest, is the firmest of all. You all in a certain sense know the voice of Christ. You could all of you repeat to me many of his sayings, or turn them up in the Gospel. But it is another thing to listen to them until you feel the power and the life of them; until your heart dances in harmony with them, and your hands itch to act them out. That is the control that liberates, and the release that controls; that is the profoundest happiness.[17]

This positive silence is not always easy to attain, and there is a paradox that for many the easiest way into letting go of words is through words themselves. It may be that a short sentence regularly repeated, like the Jesus prayer, 'Lord Jesus Christ, Son of the living God, have mercy on me a sinner', provides the regular rhythm which allows us to let go of other words and to hold the mind in the presence of Christ. For many purposes words are sharp and precise instruments for rigorous thought and accurate communication, but words can be seductive, and our use of them in prayer should be so disciplined that we use them as the means of entering into the silence of God.

Prayer must always start from and be centred in the presence and activity of God. Prayer is the movement of the heart: it is the appropriation into our very being of the initiative of God. We should not think of ourselves as struggling to pray so much as responding to the welcoming love of God. In a church which is showing signs of putting too much emphasis on *our* faith and *our* witness, it is vital to keep in mind that the initiative is God's: we do no more than – but no less than – respond, and appropriate to ourselves what God has already done for us. Prayer is grounded in recognising that God has long been at work in his world and he is inviting us to join in that work of his. Christ prays continually and invites us to take part in that continuing prayer of his.

If we walk along beside a swiftly flowing river, there is some basic human instinct which invites us to throw something in – perhaps a stone which plops heavily to the river bed, or a stick which is carried downstream, hesitating occasionally as it is caught by a boulder or stilled in a pool. Our prayers are like sticks and stones cast into the continuously flowing river of Christ's prayer. We may throw in the dead weight of a self-centred prayer which sinks straight to the river bed and which even the flow of Christ's prayer cannot take with it. We can cast in a stick, which, light and fragile though it is, and only floating on the surface of life, can be taken on by the strength and firmness of the persistent flow of Christ's prayer in the heavens. We might almost say it is not we who pray: it is Christ who really prays, and his Spirit takes us and encourages us to join in the continuous intercession that he embodies and expresses. Inadequate pictures such as these help us to see that the initiative and persistence is God's, and our job is to respond and to appropriate what God has already done and is still doing for us.

Dietrich Bonhoeffer wrote in his meditations on the psalms:

If we ask how we should begin life with God, the Scripture answers that God has long since begun life with us. If we ask what we can do for God, we hear what God has done for us. If we ask how we can live without sin before God, the forgiveness of all sins in Jesus Christ is announced to us. If we direct our glance forward to our future deeds, God's word calls us back to the past and says, Remember. Only when we acknowledge that the decision has already taken place, the beginning has already been made, the deed already done, and done by God; only when we are met by the decision, the beginning, God's deed, and know that we are drawn into it can we hear the commandment of God as the law of life for those for whom God long since has done everything.[18]

This recognition of God's initiative, which requires us to wait on him, is not pietism, still less spiritual inertia. Bonhoeffer, for all his insistence on the priority and initiative of God, was no passive member of the church, but dangerously put himself at risk for the Christian cause, finally daring to take part in the plot to assassinate Hitler. He was executed in a last desperate act by the Germans as the allied armies were rolling across Europe to give freedom. Bonhoeffer's ability to *do* so much, to be such a witness and evangelist, was precisely because he waited so much on God, and derived his strength from God's initiative.

If we start from what God has done and is doing, then our prayer is anchored in gratitude and praise – gratitude for all that God has given to us and praise for all that God is in himself. The church often highlights the failures of humanity, and there are books devoted to prayer which make much of sin, drawing attention to personal disciplines of confession and in particular to the discipline of private confession to God in the presence of a priest. These are valuable; they can be a means of deep reassurance and we should take them more seriously than we do. But we should take even more trouble and care over our thanksgiving to God than we do over the confession of sin. Indeed it is only in the context of the generosity of God that we can see our own failures in perspective and with accuracy, and part of God's generosity is the grace of forgiveness.

One of the most compelling pictures of gratitude comes from Christopher Nolan, to whom we have already referred as a powerful writer because of his handicap and the effort required to hammer out his words. In his autobiography he records (writing of himself in the third person) the experience of gratitude when he wins the Spastics Society Literary prize:

> Water shimmered on the bay, the sound of the sea golloped his voiced thanks, but he nodded towards the horizon. God, forgive me for chiding Why, he prayed, but how was a small fella like me to know that a bested prayer from me can move God to fling open the floodgates of heaven. In the company of his family he boyishly bragged but in the silence of the night he ducked his comforter in seas of creature-cradled gratitude. Communion too brought his comforter within his grasp and in close body contact he crested silent desperate credence. Communion served grand purpose, serving to bring God to him and him to servile God.[19]

Here is gratitude which must move any reader, not only because of the striking way in which it is expressed, but because this is gratitude bubbling up from the depths of an appalling handicap. We recognise that true gratitude is not just for all that pleases and delights us, but for everything, even for those aspects of life that constrain and constrict us. Such gratitude frees us to look again at how shallow much of our thanksgiving is, and how we can find life enriched by a discipline of thanksgiving which not only ensures that we use passing moments of pleasure as a way into prayer, but which uses the whole of life as a basis of gratitude to God for the mere fact of existence.

George Herbert in his reflections on gratitude is clear not only that this is a fundamental quality of Christian living, but also that gratitude must be for the totality of existence.

> Thou that hast giv'n so much to me
> Give one thing more, a grateful heart.

See how thy beggar works on thee
                    By art . . .

Wherefore I cry, and cry again;
And in no quiet canst thou be,
Till I a thankful heart obtain
                    Of thee.

Not thankful, when it pleaseth me;
As if thy blessings had spare days;
But such a heart, whose pulse may be
                    Thy praise.[20]

III

The traditional and fundamental Christian method of thanksgiving is the eucharist. Here the whole Christian community in
one place comes together to express gratefulness to God not
only for what he has given to us but for what he is in himself.
The heart of the liturgy is the Prayer of Thanksgiving, in which
we pray in the strength and power of the Spirit, offering ourselves in Christ the Son of God to the Father who has made this
world and entrusted it to us. We rehearse in the reading of the
Scriptures the mighty acts of God and then through the gift of
bread and wine take part in the banquet of heaven presided over
by God himself. Because of our lack of imagination and our
frequent tiredness, the eucharist can seem a routine and unpro-
ductive duty. Yet P. T. Forsyth, the great Congregationalist
theologian, once wrote:

> When you reflect after Communion, 'What have I done today?',
> say to yourself, 'I have done more than on any busiest day of the
> week. I have yielded myself to take part with the church in
> Christ's finished act of redemption, which is greater than the
> making of the world.'[21]

The eucharist is a creative act of God which has a far-reaching
unifying power. First, it draws together word and sacrament.
The Scriptures of the church are the treasured record of what
God has done in history, and any act of worship must recognise
and use them as a source of inspiration for the church of today.
In the eucharist the Scriptures are used as a means of rehearsing
what God has done, as we listen to the Old Testament, the
New Testament and the Gospel record of the life, death and
resurrection of the Son of God. The ancient Scriptures speak for
themselves, but they can be brought more vividly alive if a

sermon or address enables us to see that God is not just a God of past history but of present reality. Yet words alone are likely to speak to the mind and the intellect rather than to the whole human being. For that we have to use poetry, art, music, symbol, movement and sacrament, so that the whole being is engaged and drawn into the work of God. The eucharist supremely brings together both word and sacrament and so provides for the total personality to be part of worship.

Second, the eucharist draws the whole created world into its orbit. When St Paul (or perhaps a later writer in the Pauline tradition) wrote the Pastoral Letters, he included instruction on how we should pray: 'First of all, then, I urge that supplications, prayers, intercessions and thanksgivings be made for all men.'[22] It is this biblical phrase that lies behind the opening words of the 1662 'Prayer for the Whole State of Christ's Church': 'Almighty and everliving God, who by thy holy Apostle hast taught us to make prayers, and supplications, and to give thanks for all men'. The meaning here is not that we who are together for worship pray direct to God that he will do something for all those people who are not with us, as though we had a hot line to God not available to non-worshippers. The sense is that when we pray, we are representative of the whole of humanity: we pray on their behalf, articulating for them the words that they do not or can not use. Similarly when in the Book of Common Prayer the congregation at the eucharist is invited to confess their sins, and to say that 'the burden of them is intolerable', this is not to be understood as an exaggerated wallowing in personal failure. Cranmer surely had in mind the sin and failure of society, and he perceived the congregation as bringing that whole burden before God on behalf of the totality of society, whether or not they were present.

George Herbert has a clear sense of man praying not only on behalf of all people but on behalf of the totality of creation. Man is the High Priest of nature who utters the prayer that all creation wishes to express but can not because it is speechless.

> Of all the creatures both in sea and land
> Only to Man thou hast made known thy ways,
> And put the pen alone into his hand,
> And made him Secretary of thy praise.
>
> Beasts fain would sing; birds ditty to their notes;
> Trees would be tuning on their native lute
> To thy renown: but all their hands and throats
> Are brought to Man, while they are lame and mute.

Man is the world's high Priest: he doth present
The sacrifice of all; while they below
Unto the service mutter an assent.[23]

In such ways we can see that the eucharist is not a private
service which is the possession of the church. It is a public act
in which the whole created universe is involved. It draws into
its ambit the whole of the world.

The eucharist draws together, thirdly, the corporate and the
personal. A priest once noticed that an older unmarried woman
always removed her spectacles when she came into church.
Rashly the priest asked her whether there was any significance
in this, and she replied that she took her glasses off so that she
could not see who the other people were in the congregation.
This is a caricature of the individualism that is sometimes
evident in congregations. Unquestionably we should make
space for all sorts and conditions of people, however quaint
their eccentricities, because everyone is welcome in this central
act of thanksgiving (with perhaps the sole exception of
'notorious evil livers'). One of the theologians of the seventeenth
century, who saw the church as essentially an 'open' society,
wrote: 'Let it not offend any that I have made Christianity rather
an inn to receive all than a private house to receive some few.'[24]

That there is room for every individual at the eucharist is
clear from the phrase in the 1662 eucharistic liturgy when the
priest hands the bread and wine to the communicant: 'The body
of our Lord Jesus Christ which was given for *thee* . . . The
blood of our Lord Jesus Christ which was shed for *thee* . . .' This
is carried through into the Alternative Service Book, although
less clearly, when the priest invites the congregation to receive
communion: 'Receive the body of our Lord Jesus Christ which
he gave for *you*, and his blood which he shed for *you*.' Modern
English does not provide for any distinction between the individual and corporate 'you', but clearly the intention here is that
Christ's body and blood were given for each and every individual
together, not just for the generality of people without recognition of the particular people present.

Nonetheless the eucharist is essentially a corporate act. The
whole people of God come together and offer themselves as a
corporate body, recognising that the strength and vitality of the
church comes from Christians working together in the one body
of Christ. St Paul was explicit about this in his letter to the
factional congregation in Corinth,[25] insisting that they recognise
that they complement one another. It is equally clear from his

careful use of the word 'saints' in his letters, a word which is almost invariably used in the plural, indicating that we can be saints only as we are part of the whole community. Similarly it is often commented that the prayer which Jesus taught his disciples to use is a corporate prayer in which the word 'me' or 'my' does not appear. The eucharist is an occasion when the individual and the corporate find their completion in one another.

Fourthly, the eucharist pulls together the past and the future. Because it is referred to as the Lord's Supper, the implication is that the eucharist is a re-enactment of Jesus' last supper with his disciples on the Thursday evening before his betrayal. That is undoubtedly one aspect of the eucharist, but it is equally an anticipation of the final banquet in heaven when God's work will have been totally concluded: the eucharist is an appetiser for this eternal festival. The point can be expressed in different terms by recognising that although the eucharist has historical roots in the crucifixion of Jesus into whose sacrifice we are drawn, it also commemorates the resurrection, which is God's decisive act of recreation, bringing his future into the present. Harry Williams makes the point like this:

> Might it not be more profitable to think of the consecrated bread and wine as being the physical universe made new in miniature so that it becomes (as the whole creation is ultimately destined to become) the instrument of Christ's presence and power – that is, his risen and glorified body? Just as finally, in the new heaven and the new earth Christ will fill *all* things, so now, in anticipation of that divine act of renewal, he fills the consecrated bread and wine. They do not cease to be bread and wine. They do not change into something different from themselves. But when first brought to the altar they belong to the present world in which nature is not yet fully or finally gathered up in Christ. Then, as the service of Holy Communion proceeds, they are *transferred* into the new world where nature, recreated, is in the fullest sense the Body of our Lord Jesus Christ because he fills it wholly and it is gathered up fully in him.[26]

The eucharist also draws together prayer and action. At each eucharist there should be recognition that we come as the working people we are, and it is that work that we offer to God. Equally we go out from the eucharist to realise, in the strict sense of making real, what we have perceived and said in the act of worship. In some churches it is the practice for the communicant to receive the bread straight into the mouth. That is an entirely acceptable practice, but it misses a powerful piece of symbolism when hands are held up to receive the bread of life. This is the ancient practice. St Cyril of Jerusalem taught his confirmation candidates: 'Make your left hand a throne for your right as for that which is to receive a King; and hollowing the palm, receive the body of Christ, saying over it the Amen.' As those hands are held up they are a vivid expression of individuality and offering. There are the grubby hands of the adolescent, the biro marked hands of the forgetful, the gnarled hands of the working man, the delicate hands of the artist. There are hands which have been violent, or which have been sensuous, or helpful, and there are hands hesitantly held out in hope and expectation. Each pair of hands expresses what the person does, and it is as people of action that we come together at the eucharist.

Jeremy Taylor is wise enough to see that our devotions cannot stop in the sanctuary but have to be taken into the world of our ministry:

> He that gives alms to the poor, takes Jesus by the hand; he that patiently endures injuries and affronts, helps him to bear the cross; he that comforts his brother in affliction, gives an amiable kiss of peace to Jesus; he that bathes his own and his neighbour's sins in tears of penance and compassion, washes his Master's feet: we lead Jesus into the recesses of our heart by holy meditations and we enter into his heart when we express him in our actions.[27]

Finally we note that the eucharist is above all else the occasion when heaven and earth are drawn together by the action of God. The eucharist is not just a domestic church service: it is an enactment of public truth. There we are exposed to the whole action of God and to the totality of creation. John V. Taylor wrote some years ago:

> So many of our eucharists fall short of the glory of God because, while purporting to concentrate on the Real Presence of Christ, they seem to be oblivious to the real presence of men, either in the worshipping family or in the world around. To present oneself to God means to expose oneself, in an intense and vulnerable awareness, not only to him but to all that is.[28]

Today men and women of any and every description join with angels and archangels and all the company of heaven in proclaiming the holiness of God. They hear what God has done through his creating of this world, transforming it, and inspiring his people, and in the creative strength of God those people daringly present themselves for his further work. God gives them his life and his life-blood so that we may evermore dwell in him and he in us.

IV

The seventeenth-century Anglican divines based their theology, not least their theology of the eucharist, on the sentence from Scripture (King James version), 'If any man be in Christ, he is a new creature'.[29] In this context, one of the most influential of those theologians, Jeremy Taylor, wrote more than once of the eucharist:

> This is the sum of the greatest mystery of our religion; it is the copy of the passion, and the ministration of the great mystery of our redemption.[30]

He also wrote of the eucharist: 'Nothing else but the actual enjoying of heaven is above it.'[31]

The eucharist, and all prayer, much of which finds its roots in that sacrament, provide us with the setting in which we rehearse the acts of God throughout history and so are drawn today to enter into the unifying work of God. At the eucharist especially we pray that we may evermore dwell in him and he in us. The more we are drawn into him, the more he is in us to do his unifying work in the world.

Notes

1. Alan Ecclestone (incorrectly spelt in the original publication), *On Praying* (Prism Pamphlet No 34). Subsequently Ecclestone wrote a more substantial book on prayer, *Yes to God* (Darton, Longman and Todd, 1975).
2. Tim Gorringe, *Alan Ecclestone* (Cairns Publications, 1994), p. 141.
3. Ecclestone, *On Praying*, p. 3.
4. Psalm 118:23, 24 (BCP).
5. Psalm 69:1, 2 (BCP).
6. Psalm 51:1–3 (BCP).
7. Psalm 31:6 (BCP); see also Luke 23:46.
8. Psalm 37:5, 7 (BCP).
9. Ecclestone, *On Praying*, p. 6.
10. Gerard Hughes, *God of Surprises* (Darton, Longman and Todd, 1985), p. 48f.

11. George Eliot, *Daniel Deronda* (1874–6), chapter 28.
12. Dag Hammarsjköld, *Markings* (ET Faber and Faber, 1964), p. 34.
13. R. S. Thomas, *Experimenting with an Amen* (Macmillan, 1986), p. 53 and *Collected Poems* (J. M. Dent, 1993), p. 517.
14. Lancelot Andrewes, *Preces Privatae, Subjects for Meditation before Penitential Prayers.*
15. Robert Llewellyn, *With Pity not with Blame* (Darton, Longman and Todd, 1982), p. 55.
16. A. M. Allchin, *Participation in God* (Darton, Longman and Todd, 1988), p. 66.
17. Austin Farrer, *Said or Sung* (Faith Press, 1960), p. 187.
18. Dietrich Bonhoeffer, *Meditating on the Word* (Cowley, 1986), p. 108.
19. Christopher Nolan, *Under the Eye of the Clock* (Weidenfeld and Nicholson, 1987) p. 59.
20. George Herbert, 'Gratefulnesse', stanzas 1, 7 and 8.
21. Quoted in J. A. T. Robinson, *Liturgy Coming to Life* (Mowbray, 1960), p. 115.
22. 1 Timothy 2:1.
23. 'Providence', stanzas 2, 3 and 4.
24. *The Golden Remains of the Ever-Memorable John Hales*, p. 44.
25. 1 Corinthians 12.
26. H. A. Williams, *Jesus and the Resurrection* (Longmans, Green and Co., 1951), p. 19.
27. Jeremy Taylor, *The Great Exemplar: Exhortation to the Imitation of the Life of Christ*, 1649, quoted in H. R. McAdoo, *The Eucharistic Theology of Jeremy Taylor Today* (Canterbury Press, 1988), p. 57.
28. John V. Taylor, *The Primal Vision* (SCM Press, 1963), p. 200.
29. For this theme see H. R. McAdoo, *Anglican Heritage* (Canterbury Press, 1991), p. 62.
30. *Holy Living* IV, Section X.6, and *Clerus Domini* V.1. See H. R. McAdoo, *The Eucharistic Theology of Jeremy Taylor*, p. 142.
31. Quoted by H. R. McAdoo, *The Eucharistic Theology of Jeremy Taylor*, p. 15.

7

Being Together

IN HIS novels Thomas Hardy uses rustic characters reminiscent of the way in which the ancient classical writers used a Greek chorus. Hardy puts into the mouths of Wessex country labourers home truths about the society in which they lived, and they contribute a light-hearted running commentary through his novels. Hardy remained throughout his life a regular worshipper in the Church of England, although his mind moved further and further away from authentic Christian belief. But his close associations with the church gave him opportunity to observe the weakness and failures of the established church, and he enjoys using his rural chorus to mock the hypocrisy he saw. So he nicely lampoons the churches of the nineteenth century:

> There's two religions going on in the nation now – High Church and High Chapel. And, thinks I, I'll play fair; so I went to High Church in the morning, and High Chapel in the afternoon . . . Well, at High Church they pray singing, and worship all the colours of the rainbow; and at High Chapel they pray preaching and worship drab and whitewash only.[1]

Hardy provides a comic but telling criticism of the disunity of the churches.

If we are right in seeing God as creating this world and engaging with humanity, Christ as drawing all people to himself, and then entrusting us with the message of reconciliation, then there are clear implications for how the church and its ministry should do its job. Whenever we speak of Christian unity, minds at once focus on the structural reunion at national or international level of a fractured Christendom. That is undoubtedly important. It is to the shame of Christians that they have allowed the church to become splintered, and it is equally shameful that we have become acclimatised to this disgraceful fact, and sometimes even defend it as reputable because we have

become conditioned by a culture which promotes individualism, consumer choice, and 'pick and mix'.

It is true that because we are human there will necessarily be
diversity of belief, practice and style; that, as we have main-
tained, is a natural consequence of our humanity. But this
inescapable diversity should not be allowed to split and fragment us to our continuing impoverishment; it should be held
within one body to our mutual enrichment. Whatever our diver-
gences, we should be ready to belong to one body which
confidently declares its common life, belief and purpose, and
which equally happily provides for differences. The shame is
that we have allowed our human individualism to fragment the
church. The encouraging sign in this unhappy situation is that
so much progress has been made in mutual understanding and
trust between the main-line churches. Many local congregations
and regional church leaders now work together not only happily
but to their mutual gain. One Roman Catholic bishop said
recently to his Anglican counterpart that what has caused many
of our current differences is not disagreement over doctrinal
belief so much as the fact that we have lived apart in separated
communities for 400 years and have not had full opportunity to
hear, understand and share with one another.

We should not underestimate the progress that has been
made in bringing separated churches together in this country.
Primitive and Wesleyan Methodists came together in 1932. The
United Reformed Church, inaugurated in 1972, brought
together the Presbyterian and most of the Congregational
churches in England. In other continents there have been parallel and sometimes more significant reunions. The fact that in
England the established church seems to have had more diffi-
culty than most in relating formally to other Christian churches
must not obscure the steady achievements by others. Nonetheless the failure of a number of schemes, such as the proposals
for bringing the Church of England and the Methodist churches
together in 1969, and the later and more far-reaching efforts to
bring the churches in England together round Ten Propositions,
has led to the general recognition that the national churches are
unlikely to come formally together until there is deeper and
surer unity in local communities.

It is not part of the purpose of this book to engage with
national and international relationships between the churches,
but to look more at unity at a local level; and at unity not so
much between neighbouring congregations, but within each
congregation itself. Unless Christians recognise within their

own local church that unity is an essential consequence of being created and transformed by a God of unity, then we are unlikely to make much progress towards the reunion of Christendom on the larger scale.

We all draw comfort from being with like-minded people. This can reinforce and bolster our confidence, and gently suppress any uncertainties that lurk in our unsure minds. But if we have the confidence and courage to listen to people whose perceptions and understandings are different from our own, we often discover aspects of truth that we have overlooked. As we have already noted, the opposite of a correct statement is a false statement, but the opposite of a profound truth may well be another profound truth. So it is not just that we have to learn to tolerate perceptions different from our own; we can affirm them as contributing to the truth as a whole, even though we may not agree with them. Truth is not a mathematical formula; it is embodied in the Person of Christ. Just as there are differing perceptions and evaluations of any human person, so there are variations in the understanding of God. Evelyn Underhill wrote:

> I don't think Truth for us (after a rather elementary stage) can be a static dogmatically defined, 'This is it' sort of thing. It is a flash from the Absolute, never complete, always suggesting further depths and further splendour as, in and through the particular truth concerned, God more and more reveals himself. You'll find, of course, lots of pious persons think this nonsense – never mind. It is the way you will be led and is all right. Von Hügel somewhere speaks of truth as we know it, as a blazing light fading off into the darkness of the unknown.[2]

Evelyn Underhill and Baron von Hügel did not mean by such statements that the truth is what we like to make it and that we have an indulgent freedom to pick and choose truths and doctrines to suit ourselves. They were, rather, drawing attention to the richness and diversity of truth and of God.

I

Let us look a little more closely at this idea that we can affirm, rather than tolerate, those from whom we differ. One clear division in Christendom is between those who think it right and appropriate to baptise infants, and those who think that only adults capable of making their own decisions can be baptised. Without going into the details of that argument we can see that it is possible for people on either side to recognise the truth in the position of those who disagree with them. Those who encourage the baptism of infants are stressing that as God takes the initiative and gives his grace without demanding a prior response, so he gives himself to children even though parents may be hesitant and cautious. They are also recognising that faith is not just a statement of individual belief, but is related to what the community understands and affirms. Those who insist on baptism for adult believers only are stressing the requirement that Christians must explicitly put their trust in God; they cannot be Christian by proxy, nor obtain cheap grace, nor be mere passengers in the caravan journeying to our destiny. Both sides in this argument have insights, and are right in what they affirm, although they are not necessarily right in what they deny. Although there may here be profound differences of belief and indeed of practice, both sides are holding on to an aspect of truth, and there is enrichment for all if they hold together.

Another example of disagreement coupled with recognition of the insight of a contrary point of view can be taken from the apparently trivial matter of where the priest stands at the celebration of the eucharist. In the catholic tradition for many years the priest had stood facing east towards the altar with his back to the people. This symbolised that he was leading the worship of the people as their representative; that he was offering on their behalf their sacrifice of prayer and praise as together they re-presented sacramentally the sacrifice of Christ on the cross. Ministers in the protestant tradition had stood at one end of the holy table, symbolising that people had direct access to God and that the minister was no intermediary; that any actions of the minister were not secret or hidden manipulations of some suspect sacrifice, but an open memorial of the last supper of Christ. This difference of view and practice was enormously, and almost comically, reduced when the practice developed of the priest or minister standing behind the altar or table facing the people, symbolising that he or she was presiding at the eucharistic celebration of the whole people of God, with Christ in their midst.

Whatever the complex practical and doctrinal difficulties, we can recognise that we are free to disagree with people without denying all that they affirm. So we should have a church in which people do not just tolerate different understandings of God but affirm them as contributing to truth as a whole.

This does not mean compromise in the sense of having muddled or half-hearted belief. It does mean that in our liturgies and in our doctrinal statements there should be some ambiguity

in the sense of providing wording which allows liberty of interpretation and so space for people of different understandings. It
is said that a man came up to William Temple and said 'I am a
passionately moderate man.' The Archbishop responded, 'That's
all right, as long you are not only moderately passionate.'[3] What
is required of us is a firmness of belief and even a passionate
conviction, coupled with a generous liberality of mind and
approach. Unfortunately the word 'liberal' has become almost a
term of abuse in church controversy, due to a serious misunderstanding. Alec Vidler forty years ago gave us a sure and
respectable understanding of liberality which many have forgotten:

> The word 'liberal' denotes not a creed or a set of philosophical
> assumptions or an 'ism', but a frame of mind, a quality of
> character, which it is easier no doubt to discern than to define. A
> liberal minded man is free from narrow prejudice, generous in
> his judgement of others, open-minded, especially to the recep-
> tion of new ideas or proposals for reform. Liberal is not the
> opposite of conservative, but of fanatical or bigoted or intransi-
> gent. It points to the *esprit large* and away from the *idée fixe*. The
> liberal temper or frame of mind is not common and perhaps is
> never likely to be. It can be preserved, even by those who have
> once possessed it, only by constant vigilance and exercise.[4]

What is missing in much of the controversy between Christians is mutual trust. Because people are usually passionate about
their beliefs, they are often passionate in religious argument and
topple over from passion into destructive denial. There will
always be controversy between Christians, as there was sharp
argument between St Peter and St Paul; this is plainly evident in
the New Testament.[5] There will always be the need at some
point to say that this or that statement varies so much and so far
from Christian understanding that it can no longer merit the
description of Christian. But many of our disagreements can
and should be held in mutual confidence that we are part of one
body serving a God of unity. Dag Hammarskjöld sees it as a sign
of maturity that we can accept and receive one another:

> Maturity: among other things, the unclouded happiness of the
> child at play, who takes it for granted that he is at one with his
> playmates.[6]

This jotting brings us back to the gospel accounts of Jesus. He
received the children without asking questions or demanding
faith. He just received them, an attitude to outsiders which the

churches need to regain in an age when many seem to delight
in putting up hurdles and barriers round the church in the
understandable desire for clearer standards and firmer belief.
This readiness to receive people is related to maturity. In the
gospels Jesus tells his disciples to be 'perfect'[7] as our Father
in heaven is perfect. But the word here translated 'perfect' is
elsewhere translated 'mature'. It is usually those who are mature
and confident in their own understanding and belief in God
who find it easier to be generous in their attitude to others who
do not conform.

II

Unity, expressed by openness and readiness to receive and affirm
those who share our basic belief yet differ from us, should be a
patent mark of every congregation. Alongside unity there is
holiness. Thomas Hardy's rustic characters again mock the way
that worshippers in the established church can conform out-
wardly to the requirements but lack inner holiness. But his
comments apply to churchgoers whether in the Church of
England or elsewhere. One character says:

> 'There's this to be said for the Church, a man can belong to the
> Church and bide in his cheerful old inn, and never trouble or
> worry his mind about doctrines at all. But to be a meetinger, you
> must go to chapel in all winds and weathers, and make yerself as
> frantic as a skit. Not but that chapel-members be clever chaps
> enough in their own way. They can lift up beautiful prayer out of
> their own heads, all about their families and shipwracks in the
> newspaper.' 'They can, they can' said Mark Clark, with corrobor-
> ative feeling; 'but we churchmen, you see, must have it all
> printed aforehand, or, dang it all, we should no more know what
> to say to a great gaffer like the Lord than babes unborn.' 'Chapel
> folk be more hand in glove with them above than we' said
> Joseph, thoughtfully.[8]

It has been part of our theme that to see God and to live the
risen life, we do not have to detach ourselves from our humanity
and our earthiness, but to be holy in and through our limitations and our worldliness. God has made us earthy creatures;
Jesus saw the truth and illuminated it for us by telling parables
which opened our eyes to truth through the everyday. So the
Spirit of God takes our fragile human nature and works through
it as it is, and he does not ask us to stop being part of society and

of the world. It is worth repeating well-known words from the second century:

> Christians are not distinguished from the rest of mankind by country, or by speech, or by dress. For they do not dwell in cities of their own, or use a different language, or practise a peculiar life . . . While they dwell in Greek or barbarian cities according as each man's lot has been cast, and follow the customs of the land in clothing and food, and other matters of daily life, yet the condition of citizenship which they exhibit is wonderful and admittedly strange. They live in countries of their own, but simply as sojourners; they share the life of citizens, they endure the lot of foreigners; every foreign land is to them a fatherland, and every fatherland a foreign land . . . They have a common table, but yet not common. They exist in the flesh, but they live not after the flesh. They spend their existence upon earth, but their citizenship is in heaven.[9]

Both in the New Testament and in early Christian writings, we are invited to live a worldly holiness or a holy worldliness. These phrases do not mean that holiness can be compromised or half-hearted. Holiness in the world is more exacting than holiness in the cloister. John Milton wrote in the seventeenth century:

> He that can apprehend and consider vice with all her baits and seeming pleasure, and yet abstain, and yet distinguish, and yet prefer that which is truly better, he is the true wayfaring Christian. I cannot praise a fugitive and cloistered virtue, unexercised and unbreathed, that never sallies out and sees her adversary, but slinks out of the race, where that immortal garland is to be run for, not without dust and heat.[10]

We cannot hope for cloistered virtue, keeping ourselves away from the pressures and allurements of the world. We are in the world up to our necks, but we still have to hold our heads high. The depth and seriousness of our call to be holy is expressed by another seventeenth-century writer, Edward Reynolds:

> The world is beautified with the power and wisdom of God; the Church, besides that, with his love and grace. In the world we have the footprints of his greatness, but in the Church we have the image of his holiness. The world was made by him; the Church like him; the world to show forth his glory, the church to enjoy it; the world a tenement for his creatures to dwell in, the church a palace for himself to dwell in. He hath desired it for his

habitation; it is his rest for ever. Above all excellencies, holiness
is the beauty of a creature.[11]

Although we always have to bear in mind the failure of the
church and its earthly and human limitations, and although we
must never make the mistake of claiming that the church is the
kingdom of God, yet at the same time we must not underestimate its high calling, and the divine possibilities before us.

III

We have to recognise also the catholicity of the church. 'Catholic' like 'liberal' has become a word of controversy and therefore
of misunderstanding. Here we are using 'catholic' in the sense
that the church is for all people and is not the possession of any
one nation or race, still less at the disposal of a group. The
church is not a sect of our making, but a gift from God. When
we are contemplating changes to our liturgies, modifications to
our doctrines, alterations to our ministry, we have to pause and
think through whether what we have in mind is consistent with
what we have been given and with its original foundation. That
does not mean that we cannot reform the church – it always
needs it – but the reforms must bring it back to be truer to its
foundation and charter. It does not mean that reforms must be
slow; but they must be considered and in accord with the
renewing of our tradition. We have to repeat this with some
emphasis because we have already noted the way in which in
our individualist culture there is a readiness to think that we
can choose the church which best suits our experience and
outlook, our taste in music and art, and which proclaims our
understanding of God and the gospel. The universality of the
catholic church is strongly expressed by seventeenth-century
divines. One of them, John Pearson, concludes that catholicism

> consisteth generally in universality, as embracing all sorts of
> persons, as to be disseminated through all nations, as compre-
> hending all ages, as containing all necessary and saving truths,
> as obliging all conditions of men to all kind of obedience.[12]

In his gospel St John records Jesus as saying, 'You did not
choose me; I have chosen you'.[13] God is not created after our
likeness, nor is the church our creation. It is the catholic church
of God; and it is not so much that we choose to join it, as it in
the name of God receives us.

IV

The church is also apostolic, which means sent by God into his world to do his work in the strength of his Spirit. The job of the church is to grapple with the world and with humanity as it is, just as Jesus, the embodiment of God, engaged with the people of his time and the culture and society of the Middle East in his day. Much stress has in recent years been put on the need for evangelisation and ensuring that church people do not think that their aim is just to sustain a church which has been in existence for centuries. This emphasis on evangelisation is great gain, provided we avoid some pitfalls. First, the risk of all talk of evangelisation is that it may be thought of as a separate activity, and as an option which can be bolted on to the main operation of keeping the church in being. That is to fail to grasp the significance of the church being apostolic. There is no escape from being the church, which is that body of people sent by God to engage with his world as it is and to transform it. The church cannot be anything less.

A second danger is that we think of evangelisation as a simple and manageable programme. But, as William Abraham has reminded us, evangelisation is a complex enterprise like farming or education rather than a simple act like raising your arm or blowing a kiss.[14] It embraces a diversity of activities and there is the consequent danger that if we think of it as a programme or campaign of its own, it will be superficial and ineffective.

Third, evangelisation is not to be thought of as something that the church does to those who are not Christians. The initiative and action is always God's, not ours, except as inspired by him. As we try to articulate and explain our convictions, we are enriched and changed. Lesslie Newbigin has written that 'mission is not a one-way promotion but a two-way encounter in which we learn more of what the gospel means. We are learning as we go. That is the only way we affirm that the gospel is not just true for us, but true for all.'[15]

We must go behind some of these misconceptions about evangelisation and recognise that the church is apostolic in the sense of being sent by God into his world, just as Christ was sent into the world. St John in his gospel has a striking phrase for God as 'the sending Father'. He refers not to God as the Father who once sent Christ into the world. He turns that precise action into a descriptive adjective: God is the Father who by his nature and being is always sending. He can do no other. As God once sent and sustained Christ in the world, so he now sends and sustains us. We cannot be other than apostolic, sent by God.

V

Our understanding of the coherence of God and his drawing of us together into his life has implications not only for the church but also for ministry. Ministry requires that those charged with the responsibility should be seen to be drawing people and things together into the life of God. Primarily they have to be seen to integrate their humanity with godliness, the earthy with the heavenly. We can be effective ministers of Christ only if we accept our humanity fully and totally as Christ accepted his and used it as the means through which to express the love and unifying power of God.

Some clergy have consciously or subconsciously cast themselves into a role, and decided that a priest or minister is a person of a certain kind. They assume that this is what and who they must become. When they discover that they are more fragile and vulnerable than they envisaged, and that they do not easily or naturally fit the predetermined role they have set for themselves, they can become disturbed or even panic. But we can be godly only by being human: that is the fundamental truth in Christ. Grace is not contrary to nature, but perfects it. So although clergy do indeed have a particular role and function within the life of the church, they are not less human than any other Christians. Indeed they more than others have to come to terms with their own humanity and acknowledge their vulnerability, their failure, their passions and their desires.

Other clergy, particularly those new to ministry, imagine that once they are ordained people will come to them to ask advice or to explain their problems or to be taught how to pray and be holy. When this does not happen, and it rarely does, younger clergy can feel that they are misunderstood, that their training is not being used, that they are a failure. They have to learn that however professional the priest or minister is and needs to be, professionalism in itself will not bring people rushing to the vestry door. Clergy can never assume either respect or wisdom. They have to earn it. They have to gain respect and confidence through their humanity and not try to rely on some mystical status, still less on ecclesiastical power.

In the last century one of the most influential bishops bemoaned the way in which those training for ministry at one

of the colleges seemed to separate themselves off from ordinary
people in the wrong way. Referring to curates he wrote:

> Our men are too *peculiar* – some, at least of our best men. I shall
> never consider that we have succeeded until a Cuddesdon man
> can be known from a non-Cuddesdon man only by his loving
> more, working more, and praying more. I consider it a heavy
> affliction that they should wear neckcloths of peculiar construc-
> tion, coats of a peculiar cut, whiskers of peculiar dimensions –
> that they should walk with a peculiar step, carry their heads at a
> peculiar angle to the body, and read in a peculiar tone. I consider
> all this as a heavy affliction.[16]

Priests and ministers take their calling or vocation seriously
and have undoubted responsibilities, but these duties are to be
accepted and carried out through a fully acknowledged and full-
blooded humanity. That requires much patience – with people,
with ourselves, and with God. Ministers often have to learn to
go slow, not least when they hear themselves grumbling that
they have to visit too many old ladies with blue rinses or bad
legs. There is much wisdom and insight in the lines of R. S.
Thomas, writing out of his experience as a priest in Wales:

> They keep me sober,
> the old ladies
> stiff in their beds,
> mostly with pale eyes
> wintering me.
> Some are like blonde dolls
> their joints twisted;
> life in its brief play
> was a bit rough.
> Some fumble
> with thick tongues for words,
> and are deaf;
> shouting their faint names
> I listen;
> they are far off,
> the echoes return slow.
>
> But without them,
> without the subdued light
> their smiles kindle,
> I would have gone wild,
> drinking earth's huge draughts
> of joy and woe.[17]

The minister also has to draw together the church and the world. He or she is charged with the responsibility of the ministry of the word, which is a work of service to ensure that the ancient gospel and the modern world are integrated, and that the apostolic church engages with the world and is not isolated from it. That ministry is not just preaching but includes every way in which the intelligent understanding and expression of the gospel enables people to become rooted in and growing in the faith. The church remains weak in its provision of educational facilities so that people of academic ability or none can grow in the faith.

Every congregation should have as part of its continuing life an education programme with facilities for people of all academic levels to take part. Otherwise many people will rely on an understanding of Christian faith and life which has hardly moved since they first became Christians. The ministry of the word must be broadly understood and implemented. Even when this is done, preaching in the context of worship remains a valuable aspect of the life of the church, and must be a priority in the life of any priest or minister. The pulpit demands integrity. Some shy away from integrating their theological education with their responsibility for expounding the gospel, for fear of offending those in the congregation who are unfamiliar with contemporary theological scholarship. Other preachers remain in a largely ecclesiastical world as they preach, and do not integrate the gospel with the world in which most of the congregation are in fact living. It is no surprise that preachers are gently mocked from time to time. George Eliot in one of her novels has a clergyman's wife referring to the hazards of hearing her husband preaching:

> When you have a clergyman in your family you must accommodate your tastes: I did that very early. When I married Humphrey I made up my mind to like sermons, and I set out by liking the end very much. That soon spread to the middle, and the beginning, because I couldn't have the end without them.[18]

Preaching in the liturgy is precisely to ensure that the life of the church and the people of God is related to what is going on in the world around them. It arises out of a deep silence before God, and the ministry of the word has at times to be sparing in its use of words. Thomas Merton wrote:

> It is essential that priests learn how to silence all their routine declarations of truths that they have not yet troubled to think

about. If we said only what we really meant we would say very
little. Yet we have to preach God too. Exactly. Preaching the word
of God implies silence. If preaching is not born of silence, it is a
waste of time.[19]

Surely he has in mind that the ministry of the word, and
preaching in particular, should never become a routine of saying
what is expected of us. It is dis-covering the truth as we move
into the life of God and back into our life of mundane concerns.
In that movement the truth of God illuminates the greyness of
our present condition, and that same greyness shows up the
light of truth.

The priest or minister has a parallel responsibility for the
ministry of the sacraments. In marriage, the confessional,
baptism, the priest is meeting people at turning-points in their
lives and can help them to see, through their human experiences, the wisdom and transforming care of God. In presiding at
the eucharist, as we have already seen, he or she is enabling
people to enter into the heart of the life of God. All these
activities are opportunities for integration, and bringing
together the wonder and majesty of God and the fragility and
fragmentation of human life.

The job of the minister is to preside over and to draw together
and to co-ordinate the work and life of a congregation, the
people of God in that place. His or her gift of grace is not to rule
or run the congregation, but to provide leadership by identifying
what are the gifts of God that have been given to the varied
members of a congregation, to encourage those gifts and to co-
ordinate them in the shared work of the church. Discharging
that responsibility will take him or her into many different areas
of life. He will first and above all want to engage with the life of
the area in all its forms and ensure that the people of God are
with him in that enterprise. Conversely he will not encourage a
congregation to be limited by and concerned only for its own
life.

The priest or minister is not such in his own right or indepen-
dently of the church. He is essentially what he is in the context
of the church of God, for ministry belongs to the whole people of
God and is not the exclusive prerogative of any one caste or
group. The priest or minister is charged with ensuring that the
church as a whole is one, holy, catholic and apostolic, as
the primary and chosen means through which God works to
draw the whole of humanity and creation into himself.

Notes

1. Matthew Moon in Thomas Hardy, *Far from the Madding Crowd* (1874), chapter 33.
2. Charles Williams (ed), *The Letters of Evelyn Underhill* (Longmans, Green and Co., 1943), p. 223.
3. Quoted in Peter Walker, *Rediscovering the Middle Way* (Mowbray, 1988), p. 3.
4. Alec Vidler, *Essays in Liberality* (SCM, 1957), p. 21f.
5. E.g. Galatians 2:11ff.
6. Dag Hammarskjöld, *Markings* (ET Faber and Faber, 1964), p. 89.
7. Matthew 5:48 (KJV).
8. Thomas Hardy, *Far from the Madding Crowd*, chapter 42.
9. *The Epistle to Diognetus*, *A New Eusebius*, edited by J. Stevenson (SPCK, 1957).
10. John Milton, *Areopagitica* (1644).
11. Edward Reynolds, *The Staves of Beauty and Bands*, quoted in P. E. More and F. L. Cross (eds), *Anglicanism*, (SPCK, 1935), p. 771.
12. John Pearson, *An Exposition of the Creed*, Article IX, quoted in More and Cross, *Anglicanism*, p. 37.
13. John 15:16.
14. W. J. Abraham, *The Logic of Evangelism* (Hodder and Stoughton, 1989), p. 104.
15. Lesslie Newbigin, *Truth to Tell* (SPCK, 1991), p. 35.
16. Bishop Samuel Wilberforce, quoted in Owen Chadwick, *The Founding of Cuddesdon* (Oxford University Press, 1954), p. 92.
17. R. S. Thomas, *The Echoes Return Slow* (Macmillan, 1988), p. 63.
18. Mrs Cadwallader in George Eliot, *Middlemarch* (1871–2), chapter 34.
19. Thomas Merton, *The Sign of Jonas* (Harcourt Brace, 1953), p. 266.

8

Holding Together

THESE pages have been written from the experience of living and working within the Church of England which has long treasured 'comprehensiveness'. Rather than comprehensiveness, perhaps 'coherence' or 'wholeness' might more accurately and happily describe that awareness that although each of us holds hard and lovingly to our own understanding and tradition, yet we recognise that it alone cannot contain the full riches of the wholeness of God and of his work in the world. To reach towards the totality of God, we have to value and treasure our own understanding and yet see that it is incomplete and needs other insights. So as we have already seen, paradoxically we retain our tradition and yet affirm that others with whom we disagree have a truth and insight that we need. In the Anglican Communion this principle is explicit and part of our way of life.

Even within the Church of England some are uneasy with this paradox in so bold a form and would qualify it to the more moderate principle that we should understand and learn from those whose views differ from ours. That is without question true, but it hardly captures the profounder and striking truth that we can appreciate and want to remain in close community with those with whom we disagree because we see that what they hold is complementary to the truth as we express it. It is this affirmation of those who differ from us that contributes to the richness of the Church of England at its best. There is always the responsibility of having to say that, in our judgement, some have strayed so far from the truth as the Church of England has received it that they are putting themselves beyond its boundaries. That ultimate responsibility cannot be dodged, and is specifically the duty of the bishops, but it only rarely confronts us. It is also the fact that at times argument against others can be so vehement and difference so sharp that we cannot get much further than agreeing to differ until the temperature has cooled and we can more calmly and constructively tackle the disagreements that have separated us. At other times there are persuasive voices urging compromise as though the truth can be some botch or fudge in the middle ground. But the aim remains not just to forbear and tolerate, but to have the grace to affirm those who differ from us, and to work to ensure that they remain within the same community with us.

In considering this issue we should not think in exclusively Anglican terms. This principle is not the sole possession of the Church of England. There are undoubtedly many, especially in the Free Church tradition, who would rightly claim to share it. The Roman Catholic church since the Second Vatican Council has been fully conscious of trying to hold together the traditionalists and the radicals. The same issue confronts the Eastern Orthodox church as is well exemplified in the writings of Father Alexander Men. He writes from his entirely different context in Russia that 'fundamental Christian doctrines are marked by inner contradictions, paradoxes, antinomies, which cannot be smoothed out by the methods of formal logic'.[1] He was vigorously alert to the tensions in the Russian church: there is the 'conservative tendency . . . strongly anti-Western, hostile to all reforms and [idealizing] the past'[2] and those who prefer 'an open model' of the church. He himself was murdered under mysterious circumstances, which is its own indication of the strains inherent in life in Russia, including within the church. This principle of holding together opposing views within the life of one community is not peculiar to the Church of England or the Anglican Communion: it affects the heart beat of every church in Christendom.

Within the context of Christendom as a whole the same principle applies: there are churches with whom we are not in full agreement, and from whom we may differ in significant doctrines or practices, yet often we can rejoice in their existence and their witness, and recognise that other churches have major contributions to offer to Christendom as a whole, just as the Anglican tradition has its own distinctive experience to offer.

For our immediate purposes in this chapter, however, we are thinking specifically of the Church of England and of the experience of living and working within it. Affirming others who do not agree with us is more difficult of attainment in the Church of England of today than was the case up to the middle of the nineteenth century. High Churchmen, Latitudinarians, and evangelicals in earlier centuries seem to have regarded their primary allegiance to be to the Church of England rather than to any party within it. Since the Oxford Movement, which began in the early part of the nineteenth century, there has been a greater degree of separation and less mutual trust in the Church of England. This has led to the development of ecclesiastical party organisations, almost on the political model, and made many people think their primary allegiance is to a party rather than to the church of which they are members.[3] Part of the task before us now is so to value the Church of England and the Anglican tradition that people see clearly that they are essentially and primarily members not of a party or pressure group but of a church.

In doing this we have to be realistic and note how the Church of England is derided and mocked when its comprehensiveness weakens and it appears to be at odds with itself, or when the establishment mentality seems so to stiffen the limbs of the church that it staggers across the national stage in splints. Over the years many loyal servants of the church have despaired of it. Thomas Arnold in the earlier part of the last century said firmly that 'the church as it now stands no human power can save'.[4] Not much later, William Gladstone groaned that 'the church of England is much more likely to part with her faith than with her funds'.[5] Charles Gore wrote in anguish, 'You don't seem to realise that the Church of England is an ingeniously devised instrumentality for defeating the objects it is supposed to promote.'[6] Critics of the Church of England have never been in short supply, and the most penetrating critics are those from within the Church of England who have experienced its limitations and frustrations for themselves. But not all voices have spoken in such dismal terms. Mandell Creighton, when Bishop of Peterborough, spoke more firmly, and too confidently:

> We tend, I think, to make too many apologies for the supposed defects of the Church of England; its want of discipline; its absence of positive definition on many points; its large latitude of opinion. To me it seems that the Church of England is the only religious organisation which faces the world as it is, which recognises the actual facts, and works for God, in God's own way.[7]

I

It is not part of our intention to launch a propaganda drive for the Church of England, nor to claim that it is better and wiser than other churches. We more modestly draw attention to the claim of the Church of England that the principle of deliberately holding together seemingly contrary perceptions is an explicit strand in its formal statements and in its life. In different contexts it has received various expressions, all of which presuppose the value of holding together different convictions, contrasting needs, varied practices. Written into the documents of the Church of England and the Anglican Communion is this continual need for cohesion and coherence, a recognition of unity in diversity. One such statement is in the Preface to the Book of Common Prayer which sets out in the specific context of liturgy that the Church of England keeps the mean between the two extremes:

> It hath been the wisdom of the Church of England, ever since the first compiling of her publick Liturgy, to keep the mean between the two extremes, of too much stiffness in refusing, and of too much easiness in admitting any variation from it.[8]

This is certainly a more gracious way of expressing the Anglican position than was used by Simon Patrick, successively Bishop of Chichester and Ely in the seventeenth century:

> As for the Rites and Ceremonies of Divine Worship, they do highly approve that virtuous mediocrity which our Church observes between the meretricious gaudiness of the Church of Rome and the squalid sluttery of fanatic conventicles.[9]

Patrick looks to a mediocrity, seemingly midway between two extremes. The Preface to the Prayer Book, in the specific setting of liturgy, looks more to an explicit recognition of two contrasting principles which have to be held together in the interests of wisdom.

Less formally, but with lasting effect, Richard Hooker in the seventeenth century worked out in more detail how the life and authority of the Church of England derived not from a median position between two extremes but from holding together three strands, Scripture, tradition and reason. This threefold appeal has received a variety of expression down the centuries. One of the more recent is in the Declaration of Assent, used whenever a minister of the Church of England takes up public office. The declaration is made that:

> The Church of England is part of the One, Holy, Catholic and Apostolic Church worshipping the one true God, Father, Son and Holy Spirit. It professes the faith uniquely revealed in the

Holy Scriptures, and set forth in the catholic creeds, which faith the Church is called upon to proclaim afresh in each generation.[10]

The wording of the declaration, introduced in this form only as recently as the 1970s, is meticulously worded. The faith is *uniquely* revealed in the Scriptures. It is *set forth* in the traditional creeds. And it has to be proclaimed *afresh* in the light of reason and experience in the contemporary world.

A somewhat different statement of dispersed authority has been given by successive Lambeth Conferences of Anglican bishops. At the Lambeth Conference of 1888 one of the tasks was to give identity to the Anglican Communion which had spread from England across much of the world. They found that identity through the Lambeth Quadrilateral (the Holy Scriptures, the Creeds, the Sacraments of Baptism and the Eucharist, and the Historic Episcopate). This Quadrilateral had originated in Chicago but was modified by the bishops at Lambeth. The modification is for our purposes significant because, as Stephen Sykes has pointed out,[11] the changes were in the direction of making these authorities not detached authorities for reference by specialists in the settlement of disputes, but living authorities that become such when they are in use and in practice. They are therefore authorities for Christian living. We shall return to this point, but it is worth dwelling on it for a moment here.

> Anglicans have good reason to reflect on the Chicago-Lambeth Quadrilateral. Here, after all, is not just a list of articles of belief, but a series of usages, the use of Scripture in public in the vernacular, the use of the creeds in worship, the celebration of the sacraments, and the practice of episcopal government. It is important to stress that all these presuppose the church's life of active discipleship, worship and witness, centred upon Christ.[12]

The three strands which Hooker identified are evident, though differently expressed, in statements coming from Lambeth Conferences, although not necessarily with the full authority of all the bishops:

> Our special character, and as we believe, our peculiar contribution to the Universal Church, arises from the fact that, owing to historic circumstances, we have been enabled to combine in our fellowship the traditional Faith and Order of the Catholic Church with that immediacy of approach to God through Christ to which the Evangelical Churches especially bear witness, and freedom of intellectual enquiry, whereby the correlation of the

Christian revelation and advancing knowledge is constantly effected. This very combination makes difficult the manifestation of our real unity, and sometimes creates an impression of vagueness and indecisiveness which others are able to avoid. Yet we believe that such difficulties are incidental to that mode of corporate life, which, as we are persuaded, most facilitates the search for truth, and best responds to and most adequately exhibits the diverse operations of the one Spirit.[13]

A later Lambeth Conference set out the nature of authority in the Anglican church in a way that has hardly been bettered since:

> Authority, as inherited by the Anglican Communion from the undivided church of the early centuries of the Christian era, is single in that it is derived from a single Divine source, and reflects within itself the richness and historicity of the divine revelation, the authority of the eternal Father, the incarnate Son, and the life-giving Spirit. It is distributed among Scripture, Tradition, Creeds, the Ministry of the Word and Sacraments, the witness of saints, and the *consensus fidelium*, which is the continuing experience of the Holy Spirit through his faithful people in the life of the Church. It is thus a dispersed rather than a centralised authority.[14]

Here there is express reference to the responsibility of faithful worshippers who are themselves an authority within the life of the church. Truth for Christians is not defined by some academic or detached authority, nor by bishops sitting together isolated from the rest of the church; although bishops do have a responsibility for setting forth the truth, it is dis-covered and proved authentic in the working and worshipping life of congregations.

II

Our concern here is not with how disputed matters in the life of the church can be settled by reference to the appropriate authorities, but to note that in different ways the Anglican method is always to recognise a diversity of authorities and to hold together in cohesion perceptions and practices which can all too easily spin away from one another as if propelled by some spiritual centrifugal force. That diversity of authority has to be recognised not just in matters of faith and order but in the day to day life of ordinary Christians. In other words, diversity of authority relates not only to *truth*, but to the *way* and the *life*.

One of the primary ways in which the Church of England held together until the late nineteenth century was through people of widely different convictions using a common liturgy. In fact it is likely that there was a greater diversity of liturgy than is now commonly supposed, but nonetheless for a long period many were held in a common life by using the Book of Common Prayer even if their use and understanding of it varied almost beyond recognition.

Since the authorisation in England in 1980[15] of the Alternative Service Book with its provision for a variety of liturgies and for variation within each of those orders of service, there is no longer the same awareness of being held together by a common liturgical text, and people have looked for other ways of securing the unity of the Church of England. In some quarters there has grown up pressure for greater doctrinal unity, as if to compensate for increased liturgical variation. The irony is that there used to be doctrinal variation held together by a common liturgy; now there is a demand for liturgical variation held together by a doctrinal unity. Such a move would reverse Anglican practice, and would miss or even deny what has been an effective part of our method.

This variety in orders of service since the introduction of the Alternative Service Book occasions another concern about spiritual vitality in the life of the church. The introduction of the ASB and of a variety of modern translations of the Bible have undoubtedly been part of a renewal of the Church of England, but there is a price to be paid. What is now at risk is that a new generation is growing up with little working knowledge or insider dealing with the Book of Common Prayer, or with other set texts and translations. In an American symposium published recently, P. Stevick has written: 'Unmistakably, we make the Prayer Book. Yet in a profounder sense the Prayer book makes us. We are not so much its parents as its grateful children.'[16] Our liturgies shape us and provide us with words and phrases which by repeated use over a period of time stick in the mind of worshippers. Many will have had the experience of being seriously ill or in some crisis when books and people are not to hand. It is at such times that words regularly used in worship will come back into the mind and form the essence and vitality of our prayer. If we have lost our liturgical memory we shall be spiritually impoverished. There is need for a commonality in the different liturgies and Bible translations that are used, and furthermore the language needs to be not just understandable but memorable.

In the Book of Common Prayer and in the more recent Anglican liturgies effort has been made to allow the words to be patient of different understandings. This is sometimes pilloried as fudging and shameful ambiguity. That is to misunderstand. The richness of a church which recognises that there is more than one insight and understanding on any issue is enhanced when words are used that allow people of diverse views to worship and live together. There is indeed an ambiguity which is sloppy or a fudge, but in the context of worship there is studied ambiguity which deliberately provides for diversity.

In the Preface to the Book of Common Prayer to which we have referred there is reference to the Church of England keeping the mean between the two extremes. This could mean a moderate balance or an inoffensive median, midway between extremes. Equally it can mean a bold effort to hold the truth in both extremes. In the seventeenth century one writer spelt out the significance of 'moderation':

> Moderation is the silken string running through the pearl chain of all virtues . . . Moderation is not an halting betwixt two opinions, when the thorough-believing of one of them is necessary to salvation. No pity is to be shown to such voluntary cripples . . . Nor is it a lukewarmness in those things wherein God's glory is concerned . . . They that are thus lukewarm here shall be too hot hereafter in that oven wherein dough-baked cakes shall be burnt.[17]

We are not looking for compromise which arises from never holding firm or necessary beliefs, but we are searching for that grasping of truth which recognises that we have to hold to seemingly opposite views.

III

The strength of the seventeenth-century Anglicans in their polemical arguments with critics, both Roman Catholic and Puritan, was that they were insistent that they were both catholic and protestant at the same time, not a compromise somewhere between the two. Alec Vidler, in his book on F. D. Maurice, takes this understanding further. Maurice, Vidler says, was searching for 'a principle, which is a not a compromise between them, but which is implied in both, and of which each is bearing witness':

Maurice was not advocating the *via media*, at least as that is often understood. The English Church does not stand on 'an invisible equatorial line between Romanism and Protestantism'. She is not half Catholic and half Protestant, but 'most Catholic when she is most Protestant'. It is a union of opposites, not a mere balance of opinions, that we find in the Anglican formularies, and that is remarkably represented by Hooker.[18]

Maurice here did not allow his thinking to develop into any arrogant pride in Anglicanism. On the contrary, he said that English churchmen will prize their own history,

> not because it separates us from men to the left and to the right, but because it enables us to do each justice; not because it gives us the right to despise either, but the privilege of learning from both; not because it tempts us to copy portions of the systems of the one or the other, but because we can see from it that each has something better than a system; not because it cherishes in us a love of theoretical wavering, but because it provides us with a basis of practical certainty; not because it makes us satisfied with our exclusive nationality, but because by not abandoning that nationality, we become witnesses of a bond and a centre for all.[19]

Those are both proud and humble words and should be characteristic of the true Anglican who knows that not only within his own church does he affirm the contribution of others with whom he cannot agree, but within Christendom as a whole he makes a parallel affirmation.

IV

We return to consider in some more detail the sources of nourishment in the spiritual life that Hooker indicated – Scripture, tradition and reason – which have to be held together.

Our Scriptures uniquely reveal the Christian faith. They are not themselves that faith, but reveal it. Nor are they in strict terms the Word of God: the Word of God is Christ himself who is the embodiment of God, the mind and being of God expressed in the language of human idiom. So we do not worship the Bible, but we cannot worship for long without the Bible.

It is right and creative to approach the Scriptures critically and with all the resources of contemporary scholarship, but in doing that we must not lose sight of the religious nature and authority of the Bible. Lady Jane Grey, aged 16, writing shortly

before her execution to her youngest sister used these words
about the Bible: 'It will teach you to live and learn you to die.'
The Bible is not just the object of intellectual study and criticism, but a source of nourishment for living and dying. And we
have to avoid always returning to those parts of the Bible which
especially appeal to us and are congenial. Without slavishly
reading the whole Bible through from beginning to end as
though strange precepts in Leviticus were of equal value with
the teaching of Jesus recorded in the gospels, nonetheless we
must be prepared to grapple with those parts of the Scriptures
which we may be avoiding because they disturb. Raymond
Brown has written that 'in our present state of divided Christianity, instead of reading the bible to assure ourselves that we
are right, we would do better to read it to discover where
we have not been listening'.[20]

Nor can we use bits of the Bible like guided missiles in
controversy as though any one verse provided a perfect knock-
down argument. It is salutary to recognise that the New Testament writers were, to our minds, rather inaccurate in their use
of the Old Testament. St Paul could write 'as Scripture says', but
we are left guessing what passage he may have had in mind,[21]
and he seems to be quoting either from memory, and from
unreliable memory at that, or more likely using the general
sense of Scripture rather than any specific or limited text. Some
sentences do strike us with special force and stick in the
memory. We can treasure such texts, but we have to recognise
that there may be other sentences which need to be memorised
alongside them as complementing the truth. Although we are
right to use our analytical and critical skills in reading the Bible
in order to grapple with its full meaning, in the end it is not we
who criticise the Bible, but the Bible which judges us.

Our faith is uniquely revealed in the Scriptures, but they have
to be related to tradition. The Scriptures are not twentieth-
century documents and have to be understood in context. To
say that is not to downgrade the Bible nor to question its
authority, but to recognise its context: within the tradition of
the church, but shaping that tradition. Richard Harries puts it
simply but accurately like this:

> A possible analogy for the relationship between scripture and
> tradition is suggested by a selection for an art exhibition. The
> judges sit there as picture after picture comes before them. They
> judge some worthy of inclusion, others not up to standard. Then
> a masterpiece appears. At first they are doubtful of it. They are

not sure whether it is a very good picture or a very bad one. Eventually they come to a consensus that it should be hung. In the ensuing weeks the picture gains critical favour. Rapidly it finds a place in the canon of great English painting. That picture, once itself judged, becomes a standard for other works. This was in fact true, though unrecognised, when it was first submitted. The judges were evaluating it, but in a profound sense it was their critical sense that was judged. They were being asked as it were, to recognise the intrinsic worth of a picture which though it was part of the tradition of English painting would in fact call that tradition into question and shape its future course.[22]

Here then is a model for the relationship, the interaction between Scripture and tradition: Scripture emerging from within the tradition, yet shaping it, setting a gold standard.

Tradition is often used as if it were static – 'the faith once for all delivered to the saints'.[23] Just as Scripture is sometimes used in debate as a guided missile, tradition is sometimes thought of as a rampart. But tradition is living and dynamic. Edward Robinson has said that 'an inheritance is what the dead have chosen to leave the living: the living have no choice in what they receive. A tradition, on the other hand, is what the living think to be worth preserving from the work of the dead.'[24] John Habgood makes the same point more crisply: 'Tradition is the living faith of the dead: traditionalism is the dead faith of the living.'[25]

Perhaps we can make the point equally well by recalling that at the heart of our historic tradition is the resurrection. That is the bedrock. In historical terms resurrection is the raising by God of the dead body of Jesus, and a new life and future beginning. What happened once in fact and history is true and effective for all time: resurrection is the creation of new and future life. It is God rolling away the stones that block our minds, shifting rocks of obstinacy, raising the dead and opening our minds to God's new future. So at the heart of our past is openness to the future. So tradition is not and cannot be static and fixed. We are in the firm, steady hands of the living creative God and being true to past tradition is to be made open to the future.

Reason is also a source of spiritual nourishment. In the course of Anglican history this element in Hooker's threefold cord has been given a variety of interpretations. By reason Hooker meant a divinely implanted faculty which enabled us to apprehend truth whether in nature or in Scripture. Later writers extended this and saw, as Bishop McAdoo has pointed out, that reason 'was the human characteristic and that its sphere was not simply speculation but the whole range of human activities'.[26] Bishop Kenneth Stevenson similarly points out that the development of thought in relation to reason that took place in the seventeenth century and after meant that reason has the added dimension of revelation, partly mediated through experience: 'Reason becomes the means whereby the divine and the human worlds are united, through which sense can imaginatively be made of them.'[27] By an appeal to reason today we do not mean to rely on rationalisation or logic. We mean that reflective and critical experience must be part of our authentic working out of our faith.

Reason is a divine gift to humanity for apprehending the truth revealed by God whether in nature or by the action of Christ, or in Scripture. In St John's gospel the prologue makes it clear that divine reason or *logos* permeates the whole of creation. The divine reason is a principle of order and intelligibility in the universe as it has been created. St Paul argued[28] that even non-believers had enough endowment of reason to see the fundamental natural truths of life. Although any human faculty can be corrupt and misused, yet this supreme gift of God to humanity is surely an essential part of our being which we use by the grace of God to discern truth, life and a way forward into God.

So reason is not just clear thinking and sound scholarship, but includes experience.[29] Unless our belief in God roots in the firm soil of experience and daily living it will not and cannot flourish. In the New Testament itself we see fundamental truths being modified and reinterpreted as they are taken into the area of fragile human reality.[30] As we noted earlier, the Lambeth Conference of 1948 set out the place of the *consensus fidelium* and the witness of the saints. This is but another way of saying that unless and until the whole people of God have earthed doctrines and credal statements in the rough soil of experience we cannot be sure that our doctrines and beliefs are healthy plants for spiritual nourishment and not flamboyant flowers for ecclesiastical decoration.

V

In trying to set out something of the Anglican experience we have drawn on writers of earlier periods. That in itself is a reminder of the Anglican tradition. Few people today seem to have much knowledge of that tradition. In part this may be because many now in the Church of England, and for that matter in its ministry, are new Christians. They have found a Christian faith and life only in recent years – and that fact alone is cause for encouragement: the Church of England, like other major churches, is breaking new ground. But the consequence is that these new Christians have not yet had the time or the space to recognise the richness of the inheritance into which they have entered. Surely all of us need to take our past seriously in order to have a future. In her fascinating book giving an account of the efforts of the Palestinians to obtain recognition in the state of Israel, Hanan Ashrawi, a Christian speaking for a largely Muslim constituency, reflects on the need for entering our memories:

> Mahmoud Darwish, our national poet, had once sadly lamented the loss of our collective memory. 'What we need is a memory for the future,' we had both agreed. Some of us saw our reflections in cracked or splintered mirrors, while others (like Mahmoud) held the magic of going through mirrors beyond the reflected image and into the substance on the other side. What I lamented then, and even more so now, was the diminution of our dream and the shrinking of our heritage to pass them through the eye of the needle of contemporary necessity and survival – the prison of pragmatism. Repeatedly admonished not to lose ourselves in singing the glories of the past or in weeping over its ruins, in relinquishing its hold over us many ended up denying it even before the cock crowed once. In our haste to prove that we were of the future, we had abandoned our priceless heirlooms including the keys to the kingdom. We could not claim a future as the orphans of time, nor could we renounce its claims on us.[31]

Those moving words, coming from a different political context and arising from a different religious setting, recall us to a sure treasuring of our past. The fact that those words come from another country and another culture is itself a reminder that any valuing of our past must not be a narrow or arrogant desire to secure our own future at the expense and cost of others. They remind us that we should recognise and value our past as a means towards offering our experience to others for the future, and for the unifying of all people in God.

Notes

1. Alexander Men, *Christianity for the Twenty First Century* (SCM, 1996), p. 47.
2. Ibid., p. 164, but see the whole chapter on 'The Russian Orthodox Church Today'.
3. See Alec Vidler, *Essays in Liberality*, p. 157; Paul Avis, *Anglicanism and the Christian Church* (T & T Clark, 1989), p. 86f; and P. B. Nockles, *The Oxford Movement in Perspective* (CUP, 1994), p. 310ff.
4. Quoted in Owen Chadwick, *The Victorian Church* Part I (A. and C. Black, 1966), p. 47.
5. Quoted in Nicholas Mosley, *The Life of Raymond Raynes* (Faith Press, 1961), p. 30.
6. G. L. Prestige, *The Life of Charles Gore* (Heinemann, 1935), p. 265.
7. Louise Creighton (ed), *Mandell Creighton, His Life and Letters* (1904), Vol.II, p. 86.
8. The Preface, written in the main by Robert Sanderson, was prefixed to the Book of Common Prayer in 1661.
9. Simon Patrick, *An Account of the New Sect of Latitude-Men Together with some Reflections upon the New Philosophy*, quoted P. E. More and F. L. Cross, *Anglicanism* (SPCK, 1935), p. 12.
10. Canon C 15 of The Church of England.
11. *Anglicanism and the Anglican Doctrine of the Church*, reprinted in *Unashamed Anglicanism* (Darton, Longman and Todd, 1995), p. 101ff.
12. Stephen Sykes, *The Study of Anglicanism* (SPCK, 1988), p. 243.
13. Lambeth Conference 1930, Report of the Committee on The Unity of the Church.
14. *Lambeth Conference Report 1948* (SPCK, 1948), p. 84.
15. The process of liturgical revision had of course begun many years before this and been pursued in nearly all the churches of the Anglican Communion.
16. P. Stevick, *Anglican Spirituality* (Connecticut, 1982), quoted in H. R. McAdoo, *Anglican Heritage*, p. 59.
17. Thomas Fuller, *The Holy State and the Profane State* (1642), Book III, chapter 20, quoted More and Cross, *Anglicanism*, p. 764.
18. Alec Vidler, *The Theology of F. D. Maurice* (SCM, 1948), p. 221f.
19. F. D. Maurice, *The Epistle to the Hebrews* (1846), p.cxxvi.
20. Quoted in Alan Ecclestone, *The Scaffolding of Spirit* (Darton, Longman and Todd, 1987), p. 87.
21. See, for instance, 1 Corinthians 2:9.

22. Richard Harries, *The Authority of Divine Love* (Blackwell, 1983), p. 69f.
23. Jude, verse 3.
24. Edward Robinson, *The Language of Mystery* (SCM, 1987), p. 30.
25. John Habgood, *Confessions of a Conservative Liberal* (SPCK, 1988), p. 3.
26. H. R. McAdoo, *The Spirit of Anglicanism* (A & C Black, 1965), p. 312.
27. Kenneth Stevenson, *Covenant of Grace Renewed* (Darton, Longman and Todd, 1994), p. 179.
28. Romans, chapter 1.
29. As well as Kenneth Stevenson, *Covenant of Grace Renewed*, p. 179, see Paul Avis, *Anglicanism and the Christian Church*, p. 67.
30. See above, chapter 3. Compare, for instance, the understanding of marriage: in comparing Jesus' high evaluation of marriage in Mark 10 with Matthew (19:9) and Paul (1 Corinthians 7) there is movement from doctrine to discipline, from principle to practice, and from insight and challenge to institution and law. See *Marriage and the Church's Task*, The Report of The General Synod Marriage Commission (1978), p. 44ff.
31. Hanan Ashrawi, *This Side of Peace*, (Simon and Schuster, 1995), p. 245.

9

Drawing the Threads Together

WE began from a sense of fragmentariness in life, and the yearning to find some wholeness, some focus for our desire for integrity, some way of drawing together the disparate bits that make up life as we know it: and we need to be held together not only in ourselves but with other people. Ultimately wholeness and fulfilment will be found only in God, and for us that means only at the end when his work in us, and all of us, is done. Inevitably therefore we have to be people of patience, and we should wait on God aware that he will do his work in his time and at his pace, not ours. In general terms we know what he will achieve in us. The fruits of the Spirit, wrote St Paul,[1] are 'love, joy, peace, patience, kindness, goodness, faithfulness, gentleness, and self-control'. These are surely the marks of the person whom the Spirit is drawing into God. But while we wait for God to finish that work in us, we may ask more specifically whether there are indications not only that we are bearing the fruits of the Spirit, but whether he is pulling us together and holding us in his life. At the risk of trivialising even the inadequate sketch of what has been written here, it may help if we look for the signs which may mark out those who are on the way towards the God-given integrity that we desire.

When looking for those signs and those people we understandably turn to the church of Christ; but when people, particularly younger people, look at the church, what they see is not always a band of pilgrims wayfaring to heaven but an institution, and often a tired and tottering institution. The church can look like the concluding stages of a game of chess: bishops will move diagonally, the knights who chair the committees take one pace forwards and two sideways, the castles have been taken, and pawns are moved around by some sleight of hand. The man of integrity who is held in the life and love of God is free to laugh at the stiffness and formality of the church, because he knows that behind the comic façade is an original building of grace and beauty if only it can be uncovered. He is ready to probe deeper. Neville Talbot wrote in 1917, as he was desperately trying to get ordinary soldiers to grasp the value of the Christian faith and the work of the church:

> Men must dig in that strange field of Christianity through its odd and in part misleading, part repellent surface: it is a mosaic of kill-joyism and Balaam's ass's ears, and Noah and Mothers' Meetings and Athanasian damns and the Archbishop of Canterbury on £15,000 a year – through to the treasure.[2]

The Archbishop receives more than that now (although it is probably worth less), but it is still true that we have to dig deeper and see in and through the clumsy and comic institution of the church a people called by God to work together in response to his initiative. Because the church is made up of men and women it is and always has to be a social institution; it will in large measure behave and react like other institutions. There is no escape from that, nor any shame in it. But it is at the same time, and through its institutional life, a divine organism, a gathering of people called by God to work with him and to be the embodiment of Christ in the world today.

Those who find themselves held by God are likely to be people who are always trying to reform the church to bring it closer to its original charter. We need not just to humanise the church, but to divinise it, to let people see that in the rag-bag of quaint people who make up the church God is at work. The church needs continually to be transparent to the glory of God, and what matters in the end is not whether we have an efficient church made up of high-grade people and with first-rate public relations, but whether the plain members of the church allow God's grace and glory to shine through. God is never limited to working only through the church: he has more sense than that. But he uses the church as much as he uses other means at his disposal, and no Christian need be hesitant to say so. But while we work and wait for the reformation and renewal of the church in this and every generation, we can look for the more personal marks or qualities of those who are moving into the God-given integrity that we hope for.

I

Gratitude for life and therefore to God is surely where we start. Because life is God-given and each day is another fresh gift from

God, the person of grace wants to start each day with a word of gratitude. The Prayer Book collect for Morning Prayer sums that up: 'O Lord our heavenly Father, Almighty and everlasting God, who hast safely brought us to the beginning of *this* day'. There are bound to be days when we oversleep and cannot catch up with ourselves for the rest of the day, when we smash a saucer, and our whole being and personality feel clumsy for hours, when the baby cries and pushes us to the point where we want to scream louder than her, when people are critical and we feel red-hot resentment and self-defence rising uncontrollably within us. We all have off days. Most of us, too, have experience of illness, tragedy, accident, handicap or marriage breakdown close to home if not actually in it. Few of us escape the pain of human living. Yet in spite of these dark and negative periods, for the most part we should find that life is infinitely worth living and that in spite of the tough or anxious moments, we are in a rich and varied world that is a joy in its own right. We should find that there are moments when we can hardly contain our bubbling sense of enjoyment and we want to hold that, give it expression, and hope that others will be infected with it.

Gratefulness is not just a moral virtue, not merely a spiritual discipline, but a release from that striving after success and that desire for fulfilment which haunt so many. As we recognise that we can never be self-made, but that we receive who and what we are, we are set free. The Christian should always be not a grabbing or grasping but a giving person, someone who salutes not with the clenched fist, which is a sign of the demand for power, but with an open hand, the symbol of giving. The first and primary gift that we offer is gratefulness for all that we have been given.

> Give, and it will be given to you. Good measure, pressed down, shaken together, running over, will be put into your lap. For the measure you give will be the measure you get back.[3]

The picture here is of a woman with a long skirt holding up the hem to form a primitive sack, and corn or other gleanings being poured into it until she can hardly stagger forward. God is generous; we are grateful.

We can spend time mentally rewriting history, and dreaming that 'if only' something different had been the case: if only I had a better brain, if only my wife had not been ill, if only I had not been so strong-headed at that moment, if only people were more appreciative of what I am trying to do for them. We cannot rewrite history, nor recast ourselves. We are who and what we are, and we must be firmly and surely grateful for the gifts and graces that we have and spend less time dreaming of those abilities and talents that we should like to have been given and patently do not possess. The sure mark of an integrated person is not only that he is self-aware and at ease with himself, but that he is glad and grateful for being who and what he is, in spite of shortcomings and failures. And we should always remember that as well as being grateful to God and articulating that gratitude in the silence of our hearts and in prayer, we can transform other people and many situations by a simple spoken word of appreciation. Gratitude can be infectious.

II

Then there is the capacity to listen and to wonder at what God says and does. When Solomon became king in succession to his father David, God asked him what gift he would need to undertake a task that was beyond him. Solomon asked simply for 'a heart with skill to listen', as it is translated in the New English Bible, or more prosaically 'an understanding mind'.[4] To live life fully and with integrity we must listen not only to the words that are spoken but to the music behind the words. We read between the lines, and we have to hear between the words, for many who speak to us have to rely on a vocabulary which is too limited and cramping for what they want to say. Many resort to well-worn phrases and to clichés because they have no better words in mind. The sadness of language that is full of oaths and swear words, with expletives working overtime as adjectives, is that the person so speaking has not acquired better and more accurate words to use. Much of this can be offensive to sensitive ears, but there is little purpose in objecting: what such people need is not complaint so much as education in the richer use of words. The person of wholeness will listen to other people with a developed attentiveness.

Listening to other people goes with listening to God. In our age of busyness and activism, most people need space and stillness if they are to discern the rumour of angels and the word of God, and they will have to create that space and stillness for themselves. We think that life today is faster, more demanding and busier than in previous generations. That is probably true, but it is of our making. Every generation thinks itself busy.

It is the fault of the present day to think and to act as if man could do everything and certainly to forget God's special Providence. Hence that busybodyness which distinguishes the religious world and prevents that depth of piety which is the result of sober, calm reflection, and which shows itself in doing calmly, and unostentatiously, not what seems likely to be attended with the greatest results, but simply the duty our hand findeth to do.[5]

The words were written in 1835 and put into perspective our contemporary preoccupation with our own busyness, which is often an attitude of mind rather than any genuine activity of life. The capacity to be still, to listen and to wonder, is illustrated by such reflective characters as Francis Kilvert, curate in south Wales in the 1870s. He goes into Clyro churchyard:

> After luncheon I spent a happy half hour in the lovely warm afternoon wandering about Clyro churchyard among the graves. I sat awhile on the old Catholic tomb of the 'Relict of Thomas Bridgwater' under the S. Church wall, near the chancel door. This is my favourite tomb. I love it better than all the tombs in the churchyard with its kindly 'Requiescat in pace', the prayer so full of peace . . . A small and irreverent spider came running swiftly towards me across the flat tombstone and scuttling over the sacred words and memories with most indecent haste and levity. Here it was very quiet and peaceful, nothing to disturb the stillness but the subdued village voices and the cawing of the rooks nesting and brooding in the tops of the high trees in the Castle clump. Somewhere near at hand I heard the innkeeper's voice behind the church and across the brook giving orders to a workman about planting some quick and privet.[6]

Here is a man, albeit from a previous century, sitting quietly and uncovering the silence. In that peace he fills the space with a depth and quality which shows up the way that our indulgence in busyness leaves us with a shallowness in life. He makes space and time for the peace of God to reach him.

The Rule, which St Benedict wrote for his community, begins with the word 'Listen', and the Rule can almost be said to be an expansion of that one word as he gives instructions on how a community of lay people are to live together in such a style as to hear God speaking to them:

> Listen carefully, my son, to the master's instructions, and attend to them with the ear of your heart. This is advice from a father who loves you; welcome it, and faithfully put it into practice.

Surely, if we did less, we should achieve more. By securing and practising our capacity for listening we should give a richness and depth to so much that we now achieve only by skating across the surface.

By listening we develop our capacity for wonder. Charles Dickens used Gradgrind in *Hard Times* to remind us of how boring we and life can become if we destroy our sense of wonder. Louisa began a conversation with Tom one day: 'I wonder . . .' Mr Gradgrind overhears the conversation and interrupts, 'Louisa, never wonder.' A horse, Tom and Louisa were taught, was 'Quadruped; gramnivorous; forty teeth; sheds coat in spring; hoofs hard.' No wonder their schoolmaster was Mr McChoakumchild. In contrast with this crushing matter-of-fact approach, St Luke in his gospel begins and ends with a graceful use of wonder. The sense is nicely caught in the King James version, when at the birth of Jesus, 'All they that heard it wondered at those things which were told them by the shepherds',[7] and Mary 'kept all these things and pondered them in her heart'.[8] When at the conclusion of the gospel the disciples are met by the risen Christ, 'he shewed them his hands and his feet. And while they yet believed not for joy, and wondered', he spoke to them.[9] It is in the context of wonder that we are more likely to hear God speaking to us.

A capacity for listening to the depths of meaning in special moments, and wondering, can open our eyes and minds to the full measure of what is being given to us. It gives life a quality and a fullness.

III

Listening, an art and quality in its own right, has to be turned specifically into prayer to God. Prayer is a mark and sign of the person of integrity, for he or she ensures that space and time are given to treasuring these experiences and occasions of significance and holding them before God. In the golden light of joy and gratitude we can more clearly see the darker side of life and of ourselves and acknowledge how fragile and broken we are. That is not to grovel or wallow in our failure, but to acknowledge it with an assurance that God's power of forgiveness heals us and makes us whole. So we are lifted through gratitude, and through the acknowledgement of our failure, to adore God for what he is, regardless now of what he has in his generosity given us.

Prayer is too often conceived as a grinding discipline, and there is no question that at times it can be arid and exacting,

and there can seem to be no tangible or emotional reward. That
itself is part of prayer. One of my most formative experiences as
a young parish priest was an incident which among other things
taught me how much and richly lay people minister to their
clergy. I had long valued the wisdom of a devoted woman in her
nineties, and felt suddenly bereft when I heard that she had been
taken into hospital because I feared that in view of her age this
might mean the end. When I went to visit her in hospital I heard
as I approached her bed that she was quietly repeating words
from the King James Version of Isaiah: 'They that wait upon the
Lord shall renew their strength; they shall mount up with wings
as eagles; they shall run, and not be weary; and they shall walk,
and not faint.'[10] Sensing that someone was with her, she opened
her eyes and saw me standing beside her bed. 'Ah,' she said,
'those words have throughout most of my life given me strength
and assurance and I have repeated them as a prayer whenever I
have been low. Now', she said, 'they have gone dead: they give
me neither hope nor assurance.' I did my best to reassure her,
but as I spoke I could hear my words were weak and hollow.
It was only later that I recognised that this great saint was
experiencing the dereliction that her Lord had known on the
cross when he had cried in desperation, 'My God, why have *you*
forsaken me?' That cry on the lips of Jesus is itself paradoxical
in that he senses the total absence of God, and yet he addresses
him, knowing that although God seems and feels absent, yet he
must be there. So this woman who had lived a life of prayer and
patient devotion over the years was, in the moment of loneliness
as she approached death, entering yet deeper into the life and
heart of Christ. Although she feared that God had now left her,
she still held on to the words which had in the past always held
her close to him, and in doing so she was ministering to a young
priest who remains grateful to her now for an insight into
people, into prayer and into Christ. Her sense of dereliction
gave new life to another.

Prayer is not all sunbathing in warm divine light: there is also
the wind, the rain and the frost of the spiritual life.

> Make up your mind from the first to ignore the ups and downs
> of the 'spiritual climate'. There will be for you as for everyone
> sunny days and cloudy days, long periods of dullness and fog,
> and sometimes complete darkness to bear ... Remember old
> Samuel Rutherford: 'There be some that say, Down crosses and
> up umbrellas ... But I am persuaded that we must take heaven
> with the wind and the rain in our face.'[11]

The spiritual climate is no more predictable than the English weather, and in a spiritual February we have to hold on knowing that June is coming. Even in the chillier moments of living we can be glad that God is, that the everlasting arms are sustaining us, that Christ has opened wide his arms for us on the cross, that God through his Spirit is in us now. So we wait at the fountain of life and are not drawn away by the allurements of passing attractions.

The old prophet was saddened by the way people looking for the water of life went the wrong way: 'My people have committed two evils: they have forsaken me, the fountain of living waters; and hewed out cisterns for themselves, broken cisterns that can hold no water.'[12] No doubt it was with such comments in mind that John records Jesus as saying,

> 'Everyone who drinks of this water will thirst again, but whoever drinks of the water that I shall give him will never thirst; the water that I shall give him will become in him a spring of water welling up to eternal life.'[13]

Although prayer requires discipline and can be demanding and feel unrewarding, there are also times of sheer joy and release as we are aware of being drawn into God. He gives us his life as food and drink; we imbibe him, feed on him, and take our share in the feast of his generous love. These moments, however rare, are worth the hard slog and the regular discipline of waiting because they engender an awareness of how we are being held together in him.

IV

Growth in Christian faith and life will come through a steady discipline of prayer, but it will depend as well on education, on being prepared for our minds to have an experience of being raised to new life. Although there is unquestionable truth in the saying of the mystics that we come to know God more surely with the heart than with the mind, yet we still need an intellectual grasp of the implications of Christian faith. In a society of increasing education, we need an intelligent restatement of Christian belief, and we must always be ready to give a reason for the hope that is in us.[14]

The miracle of Easter is not just that God transformed a corpse in the Middle East two thousand years ago but that he still rolls back stones and rocks and opens our minds to new vision and fresh insight today. Education means being taken on from our set ways and fixed ideas to uncover fresh perceptions that were latent in our minds, and to be taken on further into truth and life that we had not anticipated. Every congregation should make provision for people to learn and to extend their understanding of Christian faith and life. The gospel narratives show how the disciples came to Jesus to learn more: 'What does this parable mean?'; 'Teach us to pray'; 'A large crowd gathered round him'. That yearning to be taught is no less today.

The churches today try to educate their members, and the opportunities provided by sermons, confirmation classes and Lent groups are not to be ignored nor underestimated. But we need a fuller and more diverse programme so that people at many different points on the pilgrimage of life can find places for refreshment of mind, so that they can pursue the way, and so grow in Christian understanding. There is evidence that where imaginative provision is made for people to work at an intelligent understanding of their faith, to grow in prayer, to strive to integrate together their knowledge of Christian faith, their practice of prayer and their practical living, there is response.

V

The Christian who searches for integration will risk his peace of mind and engage full-bloodedly in the life of the world. In Christ we see God grappling with the world as it is in order to transform it. We can do no less, and it is costly. Many Christians bend their apostolic efforts towards 'bringing others to Christ'. Without question there is merit in that, even if many would prefer to use a turn of phrase which is less open to a sense of spiritual exploitation. But the world will not be transformed only by the conversion of individuals to a Christian faith. There still remains the need to translate faith into social action, love into justice and peace; and the conviction that this is God's world has to be translated into action for the 'integrity of creation' – a fine phrase used originally by the Roman Catholic communion but now more widely accepted.

Christians in political and social life will have their own principles and standards but they will always need to work with others who may not have the same personal beliefs yet do share a vision of what can be enshrined in law, custom and practice. When my responsibilities as a bishop required me to engage with social, political and educational issues in the context of the House of Lords, what surprised me was the number of those who declared themselves to be religiously agnostic yet were appreciative of those who struggled to present in contemporary terms the spiritual dimension of modern life. It is not only in the churches that there is recognition that there should be space in life and society for reflection on human values and the place of the spiritual.

We may take the churches' participation in national education as an example of how individual Christians and the churches can unashamedly take their part in society, and work with others to ensure for this country an educational system that provides for every aspect of human nature. Previous generations of Christians in England have made education one of their primary concerns. In the nineteenth century, for instance, it was the churches which pioneered the way towards setting up schools in every community. The residue of that is still with us, so that even now when the state accepts full responsibility for universal education, one-third of the schools in the state system of education in England are provided by and sponsored by the churches. One quarter of the teachers being trained are in church-sponsored colleges.

The church of today has yet to grasp the significance of these facts. We should be more ready to reclaim our own. There is no justification for using schools or colleges to indoctrinate people and compel them to any Christian conviction. 'The educator', wrote Hare, 'is trying to turn children into adults: the indoctrinator is trying to make them into perpetual children.' To indoctrinate is as morally unacceptable as it is practically useless. But there is purpose in reminding the church and society at large that the churches together, as well as individual Christians, have a firm grasp of the need and value of education both for themselves and for the community at large. The churches and individual Christians must readily concede the errors that we have made in education in the past, but that should not deflect us from reminding people of our historic contribution, of the contemporary reasons why we still have a part to play, and although there are other faith communities now active in our society, we can still fearlessly state the way ahead as we see it. In recent years this has in some measure been done in the context of education, as in other aspects of national life, but there is need for a further recovery of confidence, and boldness without arrogance, in setting out the Christian case.

Most people will not have opportunities for engaging in directly political activities and the passing of legislation, but all people in paid employment will have the chance to evaluate the structures of their firm or company and to engage with others in ensuring that they are improved and if necessary transformed. The human values that are an inherent part of Christian faith are appreciated by many others who are not of an open or clear Christian conviction, and there are often allies who will work with us as we try to make this world a worthy place for the kingdom of God.

This steady engagement with human and social issues in contemporary society, reclaiming our position and restating our part in the life of society, will achieve more than will be gained by any narrowly focused campaign of evangelisation. In the wider context we should ensure that there is made available to people a coherent understanding of Christian faith and living so that they are equipped to make a responsible choice about whether that life and belief can be integrated with their own lives. In the specific context of the church, we should provide more opportunities for education for those who long to grow and develop their understanding of Christian faith and life. In church schools and colleges there is opportunity to influence the education of the nation. In the church there is opportunity for ensuring that people in our congregations are well educated in Christian belief and action.

VI

The Christian is convinced that God values every individual whatever his skills and abilities or lack of them. This needs emphasis in a culture now geared to success: competition has been so elevated that there is now a widespread assumption that those who compete and win are better in all respects than those who lose. Those who fail – whether in the classroom, the school league tables, on the sports field, or at work – are too easily labelled 'failures' and think of themselves as such. The Christian sees people otherwise. There is no special merit in success or climbing to the top of the ladder. The Christian values excellence rather than success. Father William of Glasshampton, who gave much of his life to trying to restore the contemplative life for men in the Church of England, and who was instrumental in the refounding of the Anglican Franciscan movement in this country, but who did not live to see the fulfilment of his hopes, died saying, 'We must not mind being a failure – our Lord died on the cross a failure.'[15] It does not matter if we are not a success as the world counts success. What does matter is whether we attain that specific excellence of which we are capable by the grace of God.

In this context it is the so-called handicapped who have so much to give to us. The quotations from Christopher Nolan are their own telling statement of what severely damaged people can contribute to the life of society – and it is worth remembering that when he was first identified as suffering from cerebral palsy, some were prepared to give him up as a lost cause. It was his parents' faith in him as an intelligent yet inarticulate person which set him on his way to outstanding achievement. Supporting handicapped people can of course at times be tiring and limiting because they are so patently dependent. But that dependence is precisely a reminder that we are all dependent on one another. Their limitations are reminders to us of how limited we all are. And because one or more of their faculties are impaired, such people are living rebukes to us of how much we take for granted: it is seeing people who have lost a faculty or skill that opens our eyes to how much we have been given and taken for granted. Rarely do we dig deep enough in our gratitude to God for all that we are, and for the diversity of faculties and gifts that we have been given. Furthermore their patent incapacities draw out of us our latent capacity for compassion. The handicapped do not like to be patronised any more than we do, but a recognition of how much they have to give to us, whose handicaps are equal but less obvious, ensures that we do not patronise them but through them learn much about ourselves. The quality of people and of society can be assessed by their attitudes to the so-called handicapped.

VII

Another mark of the integrated Christian is his generous handling of disagreements. In the context of family and personal life there is always danger when we lose our cool and allow the temperature of disagreement to touch boiling point. But this need not be disaster. Because we are passionate creatures there will inevitably be times when we cannot contain ourselves or we lash out doing damage to those around us. This is more alarming when we become aware that losing our temper with one person is because we are frustrated with another, and our anger and frustration have transferred their target. Passion is a powerful emotion that does not always look where it is going. But what matters is not whether we lose our cool, but how we handle our boiling over when the temperature has returned to normal. Apology and forgiveness are godly graces.

In the broader social context, and where there is corporate

disagreement between Christians, we have already made much of the principle that it is possible to hold firmly to one's own conviction and yet to recognise that another point of view, which we cannot accept, is complementary to what we are advocating and makes its own contribution to the wide range of truth for which we all search. Vigorous debate is a primary means of hammering out the truth. Truth is not often delivered ready forged, and has to be worked at in the heat of debate. But when Christians cannot agree and reject arguments put to them, they should not at the same time reject graciousness. The saddest moments in the life of the church are those when there seems a lack of trust between those who share a common faith in a God of unity. Forgiveness and reconciliation are at the heart of Christian belief. God worked in and through Christ in order to bring back people to one another and all people to him. So unity can never be low in the Christian list of priorities. Divisions between Christians are disgraceful, even if at rare times they become almost inescapable.

VIII

Finally we return to the point of encouragement. God is a God of generosity, who gives us life, and a rich and diverse world in which to live. Christ is generous to the point of extravagance, giving himself and the whole of his life in and through the archway of death. He is the way we long to go, the truth we desire to enter, and the life we yearn to live. And the Spirit of that God of truth is at work in us today. Even if we have gone too far in saying of the Spirit of God that he is primarily the Spirit of Encouragement, yet this remains surely one of the most penetrating parts of his work. The Spirit of God strengthens us to see who and what we are without fear or flinching, and to assure us that even though we are broken, fragmented, fractured, yet the God of wholeness is holding us together. That assurance is what many people need to hear, because it can open up to them a way towards the integrity which we know should be ours and which so often eludes us.

If we think meanly of people, they will behave meanly. If we give people confidence in themselves and in God, they will grow in wisdom and in spiritual stature. Of course some reject even generosity and assurance: we have only to look at the events of Calvary to see that spelt out stark and clear. But most people respond to encouragement: they want to see the truth about themselves and to be loved into holiness. When a man and woman are truly in love they give each other a deep excitement and joy because they see one another for what they are: they love surely and passionately, not in spite of the blemishes but in and through them. God is the God of love, and his love is more reliable, more constant, more enduring than any human love. And the Spirit is that love in action in us, opening our eyes to the truth about ourselves and, in spite of that, or rather through it, assuring us that we are held in the love and life of God, not just by ourselves, but together with all others who have made this movement into God and with those who are still lame pilgrims on that journey. If this gives us encouragement, then surely it is an encouragement we should delight in passing on to others.

Notes

1. Galatians 5:22.
2. Neville Talbot, quoted in Alan Wilkinson, *The Church of England and the First World War* (SPCK, 1978), p. 145.
3. Luke 6:38.
4. 1 Kings 3:9.
5. Dr Hook quoted in W. R. W. Stephens, *The Life and Letters of Walter Farquhar Hook* (1878), Vol. I, p. 272.
6. The *Diary of Francis Kilvert* (written between 1870 and 1879, published 1938–40), for Friday, 24 March 1871.
7. Luke 2:18.
8. Luke 2:19.
9. Luke 24:40, 41.
10. Isaiah 40:31.
11. Charles Williams (ed), *The Letters of Evelyn Underhill* (Longmans, Green and Co., 1943), p. 272.
12. Jeremiah 2:13.
13. John 4:13.
14. See 1 Peter 3:15.
15. Geoffrey Curtis, *William of Glasshampton* (SPCK, 1947), p. 157.

Appendix

THE following is the text of a sermon preached at the consecration of Christopher Herbert and Timothy Stevens as bishops in Southwark Cathedral on 17 November 1995.

> As you sent me in to the world, I have sent them into the world, and for their sake I consecrate myself, that they too may be consecrated by the truth. (John 17:18 REB)

Evelyn Underhill, whose spiritual wisdom steered many of our predecessors, wrote a letter after looking through her latest bulb catalogue: 'A jewel from the new list of tulips. The Bishop: a bloom of great substance; blue base with white halo, borne on a stiff and upright stem.'[1] When many years later I studied my bulb catalogue to find this gem, it looked as though they had changed its name – to Pilgrim. Quite a relief.

The bishop is no stiff and static specimen standing at the centre of the church, but a man on the move, a leader in a pilgrim church. He is apostolic – a man sent by God through the church to the world. In recent writings and speeches about bishops, there has been much reference to the bishop being the focus of unity. The bishop is indeed a primary person of unity holding together the life of the diocese; he is a pivot of unity linking the diocese to the universal church; and a focus of unity in the church across the catholicity of time. Amen to all of that. But isn't the bishop also a point of unity in another sense, a meeting place between the church and the world? Does he not find himself at the noisy crossroads where church and world intersect?

The bishop is apostolic – sent by God through the church into the world. He is then not just at the heart of the church, a spider poised at the centre of his web. He is a man pushing at the edges, representing the church at the crunch points in society, a man of God with his ear to the ground listening for the whisper of God in the secular world, which he will warehouse as a shout.

St John in his gospel has a strong phrase for God as the sending Father. He refers not so much to God as the Father who once sent Christ into the world. He turns that incisive historic action into a descriptive adjective: God is the-sending-me-Father. It is essential to God's nature and being to send his Son. Christopher Evans goes so far as to say that in St John's gospel, 'The humanity of Jesus is not found in his hungering or weeping, nor even in his rejection, but in the fact that he was sent into the world and into the flesh.'[2] That same sending-me-God now sends his apostles into the world. God does not do that from time to time: it is his nature to be always sending. So the apostolic bishop is not a man who makes time away from church concerns to present the church to the world. He is the man of God sent into the world who has to make time for ensuring that the church is with him.

Michael Ramsey rehearses the way in which the bishop is still a priest, undoubtedly a man of theology, and a man of prayer, but then he goes on:

> As reconciler he will be perhaps less the absolver of individual penitents than one who unites people and groups and conflicting tendencies in the common service of Christ . . . And in all that he does he will remember that his office is *apostolic*. His apostolicity is seen not only in pedigree which he holds but in his role of guiding the church in its mission towards the world, in its preaching of the gospel, in its service of those who suffer, and in its voice on behalf of righteousness in the world.[3]

Thomas Merton put it in different terms when he reflected on his own ordination to the priesthood: 'My priesthood made me belong not only to God but to all men.'[4] And Michael Ramsey recalled the prophetic words of St John Chrysostom that it is vain to come to the altar in the eucharist unless we go out to find the altar which is identical with the poor brother: 'This altar thou mayest see everywhere lying in lanes and in market places, and thou mayest sacrifice upon it every hour. When thou seest a poor brother, reflect that thou beholdest an altar.'[5] So the bishop is the apostolic man sent through the church into the world to be the meeting place of God and humanity, to be a focus of unity drawing together church and world, to be the minister of reconciliation.

Of course we know this. But some aspects of contemporary life obscure it. The Church of England sometimes seems pre-

occupied with its own life and administration – important of
course; but putting our house in order is not the same thing as
opening the windows. And are we perhaps domesticating our
bishops? These days we do not often speak of the Bishop of St
Albans or the Bishop of Dunwich; they become Bishop Chris
and Bishop Tim – almost pet names for domesticated animals as
though they were ecclesiastical retrievers rather than national
guide dogs for the blind. The title of bishop firmly asserts that
he is not just a chum in the church but a man in our culture and
society with responsibility for the life of that town and county,
and in the nation at large. In England the bishop is still regarded
as a significant figure in national life and we should release our
bishops from ecclesiastical detail to be apostolic men in the
nation.

Christopher Herbert with his wide knowledge of English
literature, his interest in the arts, his command of elegant and
imaginative prose, will always be working to relate the gospel to
contemporary English culture. Timothy Stevens, with his strong
grasp of social issues and his unwavering compassion for the
deprived, will always be wanting to hold together the muddled
life of society and the surer life of the church. It will fall to the
people of St Albans and of Suffolk to ensure that their bishops
are released to continue and develop that apostolic work.

In being apostolic the bishop will not always be popular, even
with his own clergy. That is not new. Do you remember in
Midddlemarch, Mrs Cadwallader, the vicar's wife who despairs of
her husband: 'He will even speak well of the bishop, though I
tell him it is unnatural in a beneficed clergyman. What can one
do with a husband who attends so little to the decencies? I hide
it myself as well as I can by abusing everybody myself.'[6]

To be the apostolic man in the world requires of the bishop
that he be a focus of unity in another sense – that he hold
together in himself the human and the divine. All of us are
called to be the people of God, but the bishop has a deeper call
and an appropriate grace.[7] As Irenaeus wrote so daringly and
frighteningly: 'Christ became what we are in order that we might
become what he is.'[8] A bishop therefore has to be a man of
integrity, not just in the loose sense of being reliable, but in the
deepest sense of holding within himself, so far as may be,
the human and the divine.

Today two men of God are consecrated bishops. They are
presented by the church to God in prayer so that God through
his church may assure to them the grace needed to be apostles
in the church and the world. 'Ministers', wrote Richard Hooker,

'are like torches: a light to others, waste and destruction to themselves.'[9] They offer themselves, asking that their fragile humanity may be the means through which the sparkling glory of the risen Christ may shine through into our grey British world.

They are men who will pray with Gerard Manley Hopkins:

> Let him easter in us, be a dayspring to the dimness of us,
>> be a crimson cresseted east,
> More brightening her, rare-dear Britain, as his reign
>> rolls.[10]

They are men who with George Herbert will work to recall this nation to its destiny:

> O England, full of sin but most of sloth;
> Spit out thy phlegm, and fill thy breast with glory.[11]

They are men who will turn back to another poetic writer, St John, who records Christ as speaking:

> As you sent me into the world, so I send them into the world, and for their sake I consecrate myself, that they too may be consecrated by the truth.

Notes

1. Charles Williams (ed), *The Letters of Evelyn Underhill* (Longmans, Green and Co., 1943), p. 260.
2. Christopher Evans, 'Christology and Theology', in *The Communication of the Gospel in New Testament Times* (SPCK, 1961), p. 29.
3. Michael Ramsey, *The Christian Priest Today* (SPCK, 1972), p. 97.
4. *The Sign of Jonas* (Harcourt Brace, 1953), p. 181.
5. Michael Ramsey, *Canterbury Essays and Addresses* (SPCK, 1964), p. 25.
6. George Eliot, *Middlemarch* (1871–2, Penguin edition, 1988), p. 82.
7. This phrase was subsequently criticised for implying that a bishop had a higher or more significant vocation than, say, a head teacher in a challenging inner-city school. A bishop does not undertake a more Christian or more godly task than others, but he unquestionably has a specific responsibility for ensuring that the church is what it is called by God to be. In that sense he has a heavy responsibility and a deeper vocation.
8. Irenaeus, *Adversus Haereses, Praef*, see Henry Bettenson (ed), *The Early Christian Fathers: A Selection from the Writings of the*

Fathers from St Clement of Rome to St Athanasius (Oxford Paper-backs 174), (Oxford University Press, 1969), p. 72.

9. Quoted D. L. Edwards, *Leaders of the Church of England 1928–1978* (Hodder and Stoughton, 1978), p. 328.
10. *The Wreck of the Deutschland*, stanza XXXV.
11. *The Church-Porch*, stanza 16.